My Life in Comics (a Memoir)

Ron Fortier

AIRSHIP 27 PRODUCTIONS

My Life in Comics (a Memoir)
© 2019 Ron Fortier

Introduction ©2019 Todd Jones

An Airship 27 Production
www.airship27hangar.com

Interior and cover illustrations © 2019 Rob Davis

Editing, production and design by Rob Davis.
Promotion and marketing: Michael Vance

ISBN: 978-1-946183-69-9

Printed in the United States of America

10 9 8 7 6 5 4 3 2 1

My Life in Comics (a Memoir)

Ron Fortier

INTRODUCTION

What do Popeye, The Green Hornet, Rambo, Peter Pan and The Terminator all have in common? The answer is Ron Fortier. He has written stories for each one of these characters and many others over his decades-long career as a comics writer. His tales have entertained countless readers in multiple genres. Whether creating new heroes such as Mr. Jigsaw: Man of a Thousand Parts or adding substance to established ones like The Green Hornet, there is no doubt that Ron's work has had a lasting impact on comics.

In the pages to come, Ron will take you on a trip back in time where you'll learn how he got started in his career in comics. Not unlike the many stories he has written, it is full of ups and downs, though always entertaining. First though, I'd like to tell you about the first comic of Ron's that I read. This also involves a trip back in time to 1989.

When I was a kid, I spent a lot of time with my grandparents. My grandmother had suffered a stroke that had left her in a wheelchair so my mother and her sisters each took turns helping out on the weekends. They lived in a small town about two hours away from us. To me, it seemed like they lived away from EVERYTHING. When I was at home, I could get to the mall, the movie theater, a park, or just about anywhere I wanted to go on my bike. The nearest thing to where my grandparents lived was a Days Inn, a convenience store and a Shoney's restaurant.

Fortunately, I discovered that there was a spinner rack full of comics in the lobby of the Days Inn. I made a ritual of going up there to see what new comics they had whenever we went to my grandparents. In fact, I was there so often that the staff working the front desk knew me by name. One of them would even recommend comics to me that they had read during their break.

It was on one of these many visits that I first happened across The Green Hornet #2 by NOW Comics. I knew of the character because of some reruns I'd seen of the old 60s TV show starring Van Williams and Bruce Lee, but I'd never read any comics involving the character. The painted cover (by Dave Dorman) really made the book stand out from the others in the rack. I opened it up to read a few pages. I did this with every comic I bought. If I wasn't interested after reading a few pages, I'd usually put the comic back. In this case, I ended up reading the entire issue sitting on the lobby floor.

This was my first introduction to Ron's work and I was hooked. The Green Hornet had the perfect blend of action and drama. On top of that, there was something about the way Ron wrote these characters that made them seem more real to me than how many others were portrayed at the time. Part of that was perhaps because they weren't invulnerable. Within a short number of issues, Ron had killed off some major characters in dramatic fashion. I was so moved by one of these deaths that I found myself tearing up.

Normally when this happens in comics, it is usually a gimmick used to drive up sales of the book for a short period of time before the character's resurrection.

In the case of The Green Hornet, the deaths helped to motivate the surviving characters and drive the story forward. Every issue I picked up made me anxious for the next one to come out. To this day, Ron's run on The Green Hornet remains a favorite of mine.

When I finally met Ron for the first time, it was years later at a Free Comic Book Day event. I was sitting at the table next to him promoting a comic that I was working on with Felipe Echevarria. Knowing that he was going to be there, I'd brought a few issues of The Green Hornet with me. Given how busy it was likely to be, I figured a signature and a handshake would be the extent of our interaction.

What I didn't know, was that I'd end up spending the better part of the day talking with Ron about comics and storytelling. Nor did I envision that this man would take a special interest in me, becoming my mentor and friend. And never did it occur to me that I'd someday be asked by him to write the foreword to his memoirs. Yet, I'm so very much honored that he did.

Now, prepare yourself to be entertained.

Todd Jones
Writer/Editor
Nov. 2019
Fort Collins, CO

NOT A BIOGRAPHY

Dear Readers,

What follows is not a biography but a memoir. What's the difference, you ask? A biography is a detailed account of a person's life from birth to death. A memoir on the other hand is a collection of tales and anecdotes culled from a person's memories and generally having a singular theme. In my case that theme is comic books.

So don't' expect to find details of my early life growing up in a small New England town. Or my exploits in the military and things I saw in Vietnam. It is not an intimate look into my romances or how I met the one true love of my life. Those things will remain off limits in the pages to come.

My name is Ron Fortier and for most of my adult life I've written those wonderful little magazines in which stories are told not only with words but also with beautiful illustrations drawn by talented artists. Comics are an art form created here in America back in the late 1920s and today they are published around the globe.

In the course of my writing career, I have met some truly amazing people with so much talent it often boggles the mind. I've become friends with many of them and that humbles me.

All the incidents I am about to share with you are true and did happen. I've done my best to make this a positive narrative as the last thing on my mind while writing it was to produce one of those ridiculous tabloid tell-all books. For the most part, the people who shared this journey with me have been good-hearted souls and in the end I only had to change one name as to not besmirch the individual I was writing about. He's still active in the field and I can only hope that he's mellowed and is no longer the callow fellow I met long ago. I tend to look for the good as I was born an optimist and remain so to this day.

So thanks for picking this up. My hope is the stories you are about to read will inform and entertain you but most of all amuse you. After all, when they first came on the scene they weren't called comics; they were called funny books.

Welcome to my world.

Ron Fortier
Nov 2019
Fort Collins CO

CHAPTER ONE
LITTLE ME & THE OUTLAW

Once I became established as a professional comic book writer, I naturally began attending lots of comic conventions. There I'd either be interviewed alone or put on a panel with other writers and artists to discuss our careers.

The question that always came up was "How did you get started in comics?" It seems simple enough on the surface, but when one begins to look back on a lifetime of experiences it is easy to see there are many onion-like layers to any kind of answer you might want to give.

As for me, I like to tie it together with an observation I made long ago that still holds true to this day. Ask any bona fide comic book fan what was the first comic book they ever held in their hands and he or she will have a ready reply. Really. No matter how long ago event might have been, they still remember fondly.

For me, it was when I was five years old.

See what I mean about those multiple layers. Let's go back to the beginning itself starting with my parents, George and Gabrielle Fortier.

Both of them were readers; a fact I've thanked God for often. And even though their own formal education was limited (Mom made it through grade school but no high school, whereas Dad dropped out of the eight grade to go to work and help his parents financially, it being during the Great Depression) they both understood the value of having an education. Each saw reading as a way to self-improvement. They were wise beyond their years.

Okay, so back to our story.

Shortly after they met and started dating, World War II happened and Dad was drafted into the Army. He would spend several years in the South Pacific as part of an Anti-Aircraft Gun company whose job was to shoot down Japanese bombers before they could destroy the airfields the Navy Seabees had built in their chain hopping from one island to the next.

Like all wars, his days as a soldier were pretty routine and boring, while most of the air strikes happened in the darkness of night. When not occupied with mindless jobs, Dad spent a great deal of time reading comic books that had been provided by the U.S.O. During the war years, the major comic publishers donated thousands of comics freely to the U.S.O. which were to be dispensed to our troops both in Europe and the South Pacific. Being little magazines, they were easy to fold up and stuff in one's back pocket. Thus they were the perfect reading matter for our men and women serving overseas. Small imaginative diversions from the brutal challenges they encountered day to day.

So when Dad came home in Sept. of 1945 he'd become a comic reader. He married Mom that Dec. and yours truly, one of millions of "Post War Babies," arrived in this world the following Nov 5th, 1946.

Now we'll jump ahead five years and Mom and Dad are living in a nice duplex apartment owned by Dad's parents—my grandparents—Jean Baptiste and Rose Fortier. Talk about being twice blessed! I grew up with them next door. It was like having two sets of loving parents.

Now Dad went to work at a nearby bleachery, a factory that tans animal hides into leather. A dirty job for sure, but it paid the bills. Mom stayed home to keep house and raise her precocious little Ronnie and kid brother Georgie. George Fortier Junior was born in 1948.

As to why my younger brother got Dad's name and I didn't is easily explained. Mom had wanted to name me after Dad, but he nixed the idea. A G.I. named Ron had been his best friend overseas and he wanted his son given that name. Of course I'd have preferred he go with just Ron, but being a prim and proper fellow, he stuck me with Ronald. A tag that would come to plague me when McDonald's finally came along with their stupid clown mascot, Ronald. *Ouch.*

Okay, so you get the picture. Dad works all week at the factory, Mom tends the home fires with her two boys. They were never rich and looked forward to their weekends as a couple of days to rest up. Time to enjoy a little peace and quiet. As much as one can have with two little boys running around under foot.

Now keep in mind, it was now 1951. On Saturday mornings Dad would jump in the car and go off to run whatever errands Mom had set for him, while she prepared dinner (in New England, the noon time meal is dinner, the evening meal is supper. Or, at least it was when I was a tyke).

While out getting groceries, Dad would pick up a couple of comic books; crime and westerns for himself and romance and true confessions for Mom. After dinner, with the dishes put away, they would go into the living room, see to it that George Jr. and I were okay playing on the rug and then they'd turn on the big old radio set to listen to dance music while they sat back in their easy chairs and read their comic books. Again, dear readers, this was pre-TV.

Naturally, being five, I was curious as to what those brightly colored little magazines were that kept my folks happily entertained. Enough so that, like most kids, I began going from one to the other with my pudgy little hands out mouthing, "Gimme, gimme, gimme." At this point Mom would look over to Dad and suggest he give me one of his.

"No way," Dad responded. "He'll end up either putting it in his mouth or simply ripping it apart." Now there wasn't a jealous bone in Dad's body, but I have to admit he was right. That's exactly what I would have done—and eventually did. But let's not get ahead of the story here.

Thankfully Mom had inherited the wisdom of Solomon and offered up this glorious idea. "The next time you are out buying comics, why not pick up two of the same title. That way you can give the extra one to Ronnie and it won't matter what he does with it?"

See, I told you she was smart.

The very next Saturday, while buying his weekly stash of comics, Dad picked up two issues of the latest western title, *Kid Cold, Outlaw.* Then a few hours later, when little Ronnie looked up at him with hands outstretched asking for his own comic, Dad handed him his very first comic book. Now, I've obviously long forgotten the euphoria of that particular moment. Did I get down on the rug and eagerly begin perusing all those pages with their brightly colored picture panels? Or did I in fact tear the thing apart within a few short minutes?

Honestly, those details are long lost to me. What is not is the cover featuring a blonde haired cowboy wearing boots, jeans, a red shirt and a black and white vest with a white hat; Kid Colt.

And that was just the beginning. Dad would continue to buy me a comic every so often. It wasn't necessary to do so every week as I was perfectly content to look at the same ones over and over and over again.

Not knowing how to read yet, it was only a matter of time before I wanted to know what all that chicken scrawl was in the word balloons and captions. I'd deduced they were words and started pestering Mom on a daily basis to tell me what each one meant and sounded like. She only endured that for so long. By the time I was six, she sat me down at the kitchen table and plopped this massive book down in front of me. It was a dictionary and she taught me how to use it properly.

I felt I'd been given a treasure. I instantly fell in love with words.

I do remember reading DC's Superboy title at a young age and being perplexed by one single word that appeared in every single issue; invulnerable. In each story we were told Superboy was invulnerable. Okay, so I grabbed the family dictionary and looked it up.

Invulnerable; impervious to all harm. Cannot be hurt.

I spent the next week driving everyone in the neighborhood crazy by telling them in a loud boyish voice, "Did you know Superboy is invulnerable." Oh, yeah, Dennis the Menace had nothing on me.

So here's the thing. I really did learn to read through comic books. By the time I finished grade school and made it to high school, I'd graduated to reading paperback novels; mostly private eye mysteries and science fiction. It's where I discovered such fantastic American writers as Edgar Rice Burroughs, Ray Bradbury, Robert E. Howard, Ed McBain and so many others. In those days, I always had a book in my hand.

By the time I entered St. Thomas Aquinas High School, a catholic parochial school, I knew I wanted to be a comic book writer. Again, God was keeping an eye out on me as my freshmen homeroom teacher was a nun named Sister Raymunda. I would have her for three years of English and her influence on me continues to this day.

One final incident and then we'll wrap up this chapter.

At the start of our sophomore year we were asked to write a list of all the books we had read up to that point in our lives. Apparently the teachers wanted to get some sense as to where we were in regards to what level of competency in our reading and writing skills. So that night I went up into the attic where I stored all my paperbacks and began jotting their titles down in a notebook.

The next day my fellow students turned in their list. Most of these averaged about ten titles. I handed Sister Raymunda my list with 300 titles on it. To her credit she never questioned its veracity but rather took me under her wing. She was smart enough to know that she had a budding writer on her hands.

○ ○ ○

ADDITIONAL FACTS-

Kid Colt and his horse Steel first appeared in *Kid Colt* # 1 (August 1948) from Timely Comics. Originally his cover logo was subtitled "Hero of the West" but by issue three that was changed to "Outlaw." Pete Tumlinson was the primary artist on Kid Colt, Outlaw from issues # 14-24 (May 1951 – Jan 1953). Though many artists worked on the series, no one drew more Kid Colt stories than Jack Keller.

In 1960, Editor Stan Lee convinced the publishers to bring back super-heroes and change the company's name to Marvel, thus kicking off what is known as the Silver Age of Comics and with the release of such comics as the Fantastic Four, Spider-Man, Thor, Iron-Man, the Hulk etc. etc. Timely was gone forever and the Marvel Age was here to stay.

I was all of 13 when this happened and by then a die-hard comics fan, it seemed like every week was Christmas.

Marvel, while creating all these new and exciting books, kept the westerns and Lee took over the writing chores on Kid Colt, Outlaw. Artists like John Severin and Russ Heath did covers until penciler Jack Kirby and inker Dick Ayers took over the bulk of them in 1965.

The series ended in 1969 with several reprint specials appearing in April of 1979 making it the longest-running Western comic-book ever.

THE INTERIM

Remember how I said in my introduction that there would be parts of my life I would not elaborate on? Well, this is such a break in our narrative. There may be more.

I graduated from high school in 1964, pretty much a B grade student. Thing is, I was fed up with school and just wanted to get out into the real world. For me that meant going to work in a local shoe factory where I lasted almost a full year. Vietnam was happening and the news reported that the Army was about to have one of its largest drafts ever. Now the idea of being a grunt and sloshing through miles of bug infested hot jungles didn't appeal to me in the slightest.

Of course the Army recruiters had all kinds of tricks to get us to join. If you took a battery of aptitude tests and qualified for a particular job, it would be guaranteed to you before you enlisted. After a year in the factory and feeling Uncle Sam was going to get me anyway, I took a chance and went to take the tests. At the end of the day I was told I had maxed them and could sign up for any clerical M.O.S.[1] the Army had to offer. The top such was Personal Specialist. I signed on the dotted line, got my copy of the guarantee and then joined the U.S. Army.

I served between Sept of 1965 to July 1968. I went to Fort Dix in New Jersey for both Basic and Advanced Training, and then shipped out to Fort Ord, California where I worked in a battalion mail room for the next two years. My last year was

---

1   MOS: **M**ilitary **O**ccupational **S**pecialty (US Army)

spent in Vietnam. If I ever get around to writing about my time in the Army, trust me, it will make the movie "Stripes" seem like a very serious melodrama.

It should be noted that while I was in Vietnam, I wrote a weekly column for our local town newspaper, "The Somersworth Free Press." Mom tells me when my column began appearing, people would stop my Dad on the street and comment graciously about having read it. She says Dad was really proud of me for that column. Sadly it would be the only professional work of mine he would ever live to see.

Upon getting back to civilian life in 1968, I did two years at the University of New Hampshire majoring in Philosophy. Truth to tell, I was only killing time and really had no clue what it was I wanted to do. Oh, the dream of wanting to be a writer was still there, but at this time in my life I didn't have that much faith in dreams. Reality was saying it was time to get on with things and grow up. Start a family or something. So one day I jumped into my Volkswagen beetle and drove off campus and never looked back.

A few months later I married. It was a mistake. Whereas God never makes a mistake and that union produced three amazing human beings, Scott, Kevin and Heather. I love each of them more than all the words in the world can ever say.

Now a family man, I went to work for a General Electric factory in town. Eleven years later I got a divorce. A few years later began dating Valerie, who worked with me at GE. Also divorced, she had two kids, Michelle and Alan. Yes, the term blended family does apply. They are all great people, despite the flaws of their parents.

Valerie and I married and my writing career started to take off.

On to Chapter Two.

CHAPTER TWO

CBG & FANZINES

So here I was, three years after returning to civilian life, working at G.E., married with children and living in an upstairs apartment. I'd gotten back into comic reading as soon as returning home. Keep in mind this was still the time of distribution solely through various retail outlets. There still were no such things as Comic Shops.

In 1971 a by-monthly newspaper called The Buyer's Guide came on the scene and I immediately bought a subscription. Thus every two weeks I was able to keep up with all the latest happenings in the world of comics. I've no actual idea as to what their readership numbers were, but I have to believe it to have been in the thousands.

Via CBG, as it came to be known, I discovered such comic personalities as Don & Maggie Thompson who wrote a column called "Beautiful Balloons." In 1983 they became the paper's editors and Don expanded his workload by writing reviews of new comics. Other well known columnists who appeared in the CBG were Cat Yronwode, Peter David, Mark Evanier, Bob Ingersol and Tony Isabella. Remember that last name as he's going to play a pivotal role in our story shortly.

Now, one of the regular features of CBG was its Personal Ads which appeared in the back of each issue. These were mostly advertisement for amateur magazines produced by fans and thus called Fanzines. I became intrigued by them and began ordering copies. A fellow in Massachusetts named Marty Grein was publishing a fanzine called "The Comic Crusader" and it was great. Each had lots of articles, interviews and terrific art. It was in them that I found the artwork of a gentlemen named Gary Kato that reminded me a great deal of Marvel's Steve Ditko; the artist made famous by drawing Spider-Man and Doctor Strange.

Then there were these two guys from Canada; Art Cooper and Vincent Marchesano. Both of them artists, they were selling mini-comics under the name of Spectrum Publications. These were small black and white comics just a wee bit bigger than a pack of cigarettes. Their flagship title was "Id, Ego, Aeon." On a whim one night, I sat down at the kitchen table with my trusty old typewriter and wrote a short five page script featuring one of Cooper's characters, Freedom Fighter. The next day I stuck it in a 5 X 7 manila enveloped and mailed it to him. Much to my delight, he replied saying he liked my story and went on to illustrate it for their next mini issue. When my copies arrived, I remember being thrilled. No matter what happened next, that little bitty strip was my first ever published comic. The story was called "Pay Your Dues" and is dated 1970.

Thus encouraged, I later wrote another short strip creating a science fiction hero called "Vicon of the Skyriders" which Marchesano edited and illustrated for their next issue. Sadly Spectrum didn't stick around long and thus ended my relationship with those Canadian mini-treasures. (Note— both Art & Vincent are still drawing comics and other things up there in the North Country.)

Fanzines were not only devoted to comics. There were prose fiction-zines and one that I ended up subscribing to was "Space & Time" created and published by New Yorker Gordon Linzner. The thought of writing prose wasn't uppermost in my thoughts in those days. Still, reading the excellent stories Linzner published, I began toying with the idea that I might be able to write one myself. I'd also noted that, when possible, the stories printed in "Space & Time" were often accompanied by black and white illustrations.

I had faith in my burgeoning skills but fearing my submission would be rejected because I was a new, unknown writer, I decided to acquire some additional insurance. I would send my finished story to a fan artist to do illustrations for me. Then I'd send the package with both manuscript and art to Linzner thus doubling my chances he'd accept them both.

But who would I find to do those illustrations?

I flipped through my issues of "Comic Crusader" and decided this Kato guy might be the artist I needed. I wrote a letter to him, placed it in a bigger envelope with another missive; this one addressed to the editor, Greim. In the cover letter I explained I was hoping to connect with Kato and would he be so kind as to address the smaller envelope and mail it off to him. I had realized early on, most publishers respected their contributors' privacy and would not simply give out such contact information willy-nilly. Happily, Greim went along with my request and sent the note off to Honolulu, Hawaii, home of the talented young Mr. Kato.

A little over a week later I received my first letter from Gary. Thus began a friendship that would last a lifetime and continues to this day. I doubt seriously my career would have progressed had I not hooked up with Gary. The two of us shared similar dreams and together we made things happen.

Gary was interested in illustrating my sci-fi short story and now equipped with his mailing address, I sent it off to him suggesting he might do a couple of illustrations. He did six. All of them were stunning. No surprise, Linzner, upon seeing them, accepted both story and art for issue # 26 of "Space and Time." Gary's art graces the cover with the other five pieces appearing inside with a story titled by "The Raid on Tauron IV" by Ron Fortier.

Within the next year or so, Gary and I would collaborate on yet another submission for "Space and Time." This one inspired by the works of Robert E. Howard and told the story of a red-headed Cossack warrior who battles were-wolves. I've since forgotten the title but recall how once again Gary delivered some truly beautiful illustrations.

At the end of this chapter in my life, I co-wrote one more story for Linzner that would appear in a special book anthology called "Bringing Down the Moon." My fellow writer on that story was a dude named Kevin Anderson[2]. You may have heard of him. I've lost count as to how many New York Times bestselling books he's written.

The important thing here was my meeting Gary and what lay ahead of us in the months to come. The fun was just beginning.

ADDITIONAL FACTS-

The Buyer's Guide was established in 1971 and was the longest running periodical reporting on the American comic book industry. It awarded its annual Comics Buyer's Guide Fan Awards from 1982 to 2008 with the first awards announced in # 500 (June 17, 1983. In 1983 The Buyer's Guide was purchased by Krause Publications and changed the name to Comics Buyer's Guide on issue # 482, Feb 11, 1983. The magazine was headquartered in Iola, Wisconsin.

CHAPTER THREE

THE CHARLTON BULLSEYE

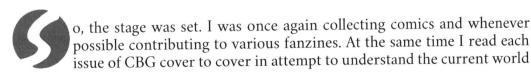

o, the stage was set. I was once again collecting comics and whenever possible contributing to various fanzines. At the same time I read each issue of CBG cover to cover in attempt to understand the current world

---

2   For those not familiar with Kevin Anderson his Wikipedia entry is: https://en.wikipedia.org/wiki/Kevin_J._Anderson

of comics while doing my best to become a part of it. Finally in 1980 a very important announcement was heralded in the CBG. Charlton Comics, a small outfit located in Derby, Conn. was going to produce what would basically be a try-out title.

I was familiar with Charlton and other smaller publishers like Gold Key, ACG and others. Most of the time they dealt with TV or movie licenses or did the run-of-the-mill westerns, horror and romance comics. And although many industry pros did work for them on and off, they simply never attained the status of either DC or Marvel. Thus most comic fans, such as I, would pick up one or two of their books when we'd finished the current issues from the Big Two.

Okay, so back to this try-out title. Managing Editor George Wildman and Assistant Editor Bill Pearson were asking non-professional comic creators to send them their strips. If any were chosen and published in their new series—to be called The Charlton BULLSEYE—then each creator would receive 50 copies. It wasn't cash, but then again one could claim in all honesty to be a published comic pro.

I liked the idea immediately. The logic of breaking into one of the smaller publishers made sense. One could conceivably spend a lifetime banging on Marvel or DC's door and never make a dent. Whereas here was a company actually asking new kids to send their stuff in. I also knew just who I had to contact immediately; Gary Kato.

Suspecting hundreds of would-be artists and writers would also be reading the self-same article in the CBG, there was no time to lose. Especially on a letter that would have to travel half-way around the world from Somersworth, NH, to Honolulu, HI. I picked up the phone and called long distance. Screw the phone bill, this was an emergency.

Even though we'd exchanged phone numbers, I don't believe Gary or I had ever had the occasion to call each other. You can imagine his surprise when he picked up phone, said "Hello" and then heard this Yankee New Englander coming at him over the phone the line.

I identified myself and the conversation began. This is a good point to bring up the fact that people from around the globe tend to speak in different styles. Whereas Gary had been born and raised on the islands, his was a very slow, easy, take-your-time patois that seemed to make single sentences go on and on and on. While being born and brought up in the cold North East, where seasons changed at the drop of a hat, I had that nervous anxiety of what to rattle off at the speed of light.

Now imagine these two totally opposite speech patterns colliding.

I'm standing there doing my best to keep my mouth shout, while Gary finishes his sentence, at the same time twisting the phone chord in a knot and tapping my right foot on the floor ceaselessly. I imagined my words the Hare and Gary's the Tortoise. In looking back at that moment over the landscape of the past, I find myself chuckling. Again, keep in mind, this was only our first actual conversation. In the years to come there would be hundreds more and eventually I would come not only to love the sound of my friend's voice, but allow it to calm me down and take things a little slower.

Call it island time.

Of course, much to my delight, Gary had read his own copy of the CBG and had seen the Charlton ad. He was only too eager to do a comic strip with me. How fast could I get it written and off to him? I told him I'd have it off in the mail to him within a few days.

I kept that promise. The story I wrote was a seven page space opera I called "Duel In The Stars," and it tells of a intergalactic battle between two spaceships from warring empires; the humans and a race of humanoid cat-people. Having been wowed with the cat-people Gary had done for the "Space and Time" illustrations, I knew he could deliver some really great looking graphics with such characters. Within several days the manuscript was typed up and in an envelope on its way West.

All fingers crossed.

As I would come to learn over the years, Gary doesn't procrastinate. Ever. The second my script arrived, he began drawing. Remember, at this juncture in our growing partnership, I'd never seen any of his actual comics work. I had no idea just how talented he was and that he would compose, pencil, ink and letter the entire seven pages all by himself. Or how damn beautiful it would end up looking.

Of course I'd been right about the Charlton offices getting flooded within days of the CBG announcement having been posted. They received hundreds of art submissions of varying quality. Some were really good but needed a little technical tweaking to get them into shape for printing while others were totally amateurish and returned to senders.

Gradually Pearson and his people began to assemble and work on enough good pages to start filling issues of the first few books in the series.

It is my belief that Gary's package with all seven of his pages arrived within a few weeks of the programs inauguration. When Pearson saw the pages, he smiled from ear to ear. Of all the entries they received for the Charlton Bullseye, our "Duel In The Stars"was the only strip that arrived ready to go to print; once it was colored. It required no additional work what-so-ever. Pearson related this to us after the story had been published.

"Duel In The Stars" appeared in the third issue of the Charlton Bullseye dated 1981. It was the last story in the comic and featured the image of a witch on the cover as drawn by one Dan Carr.

Weeks later Gary and I received our 50 copies. As of that moment, we were comic book pros!

CHAPTER FOUR

RALPH & THE FLEA MARKET

At this particular time in history, the area known as Southern New Hampshire was in no way the comic-book epicenter of the universe. But that was all about to change and no, not because Ron Fortier had just had his first professional comic strip published. Oh no, the cause of that seismic-eruption was due entirely to a couple of other young comic creators who just happened to be at the right place at the right time.

And to better explain that I should give you a small geography lesson. In this part of Southern New Hampshire situated along the Maine border are several cities and towns separated from our neighboring state by the Salmon Falls River. This body of water runs south through these communities and they are often referred to as the Tri-City municipalities. Rochester is the furthest north, then there is Somersworth and last in line the city of Dover. Think of a triangle with each of these hamlets occupying one point.

As I mentioned earlier, Somersworth was my home town. Whereas a young fellow named Ralph Dibernardo lived in Rochester and those two creative guys I referred to before lived in nearby Dover. As you can see, our cast is expanding.

Do keep in mind that at this time there were still no comic book stores in our area, though by then they were beginning to pop up in larger cities across the country. It was frustrating for we small town fans knowing both Marvel and DC were producing titles made available only through such stores to which we had no access. Eventually I heard of a young dude who had somehow managed to work a deal with a national distributor to get the exact same comic titles sold only to comic shops. Every Sunday he would rent several tables at a giant Fleamarket in the nearby village of Newington and there sell these exclusive comics.

Remember that river winding its way southward. Well after leaving Dover, it meanders its way through little old Newington before reaching the well known historical town of Portsmouth NH and there was embraced by the cold waters of the Atlantic Ocean.

The building that housed the Sunday Newington Fleamarket was huge with several hundred vendors selling all the things you'd expect to find at your average market from old antiques, hardware tools, homemade crafts, canned goods and assorted junk. And at three tables to the right upon entering the cavernous building was this lanky guy named Ralph Dibernardo and dozens of brand new comics from all the publishers. Again, the very comics we fans living there couldn't find at the local drug store spinner racks.

Naturally I wasted no time in driving there to see if the stories were true and was delighted to learn they had been so. Meeting Ralph was a pleasure and we easily became good friends. He couldn't have been much older than twenty. He was genuinely excited about my own passion for comics and especially upon hearing

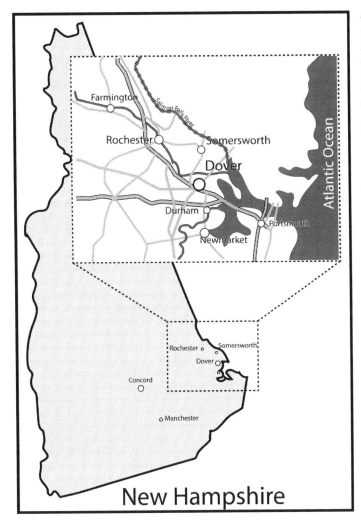

New Hampshire

of my recent success with the Charlton Bullseye program. Through Ralph I met many other local comic fans from the Tri-City area and all of us getting together at the Fleamarket Sunday mornings soon became a happy routine. Among these were Larry Young, Ken McFarlane, Rich Woodall, Matt Talbot and many, many others. Ralph made it no secret that if he could build his client base at the Fleamarket over a year or two, then his ultimate goal was to open a comic-shop in the area. Of course all of us were extremely excited about that idea.

One of the things people soon learned upon getting to know Ralph was that he was a go-getter; a totally self-motivated individual who wasn't afraid of hard work to achieve his life's dreams.

Thus it really didn't surprise me all that much that within several years of starting up his Flea Market business, Ralph began talking about putting on a mini comic convention. He had started talking to various public venues in the area and doing his homework as to how much it would cost to rent a hall etc. for a one day event. Then one day he informed me that he had reached out to a New England based comic book fellow named Joe Blowhard who had begun producing his own science-fiction comic book called "The Abandoned."

(Joe Blowhard is not his real name. It has been changed for reasons that will soon become obvious.)

Having bought several copies of this amateur comic via mail, I was impressed by the caliber of artwork. Blowhard was a really good artist. The story itself was mediocre at best and Blowhard relied on his ability to draw full-bosomed sexy space girls to sell his book…and it did. Enough so that he was considered at that time a rising star on the comic horizon.

So Ralph had invited Joe Blowhard to come and be his premier guest at his first ever one day comic gathering.

And then he asked me if I'd be his second guest. I was both surprised and flattered. Truth is mostly all the fifty copies of the comic Charlton had sent me were long gone. I'd passed them out to friends and family. The few I had left I wasn't about to part with. But then again, from projects in various fanzines, I had accrued some truly beautiful artwork from such artists as Gary Kato and these I could easily put on display and show off to fans who attended the show.

I happily agreed to be Ralph's second guest.

"So where are you going to hold the thing?" I asked.

"At the Howard Johnson's at the Portsmouth Traffic Circle."

Time for another lesson on the geography of this setting. Imagine you are in Massachusetts and driving northward; your destination Maine. You most likely would travel up U.S. Route 95 which would then bring you to the Portsmouth Traffic Circle.

Now upon entering the circle (or round-about as it is known in other places) to veer to the right and take exit # 1 and you will find yourself going into the city itself. If we continue around as if bisecting the actual circle, then you are shooting north and will soon pick up U.S. Route 1 which hugs the Maine coast passing such beautiful seacoast resorts as Ogunquit, York, Wells, and dozens more. It really is a beautiful, scenic highway in the summer months.

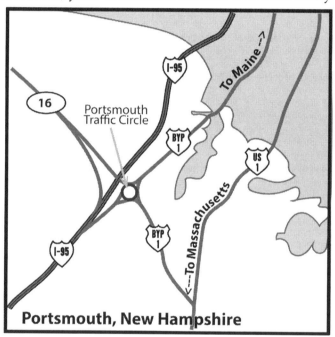

Portsmouth, New Hampshire

Whereas if you complete 75% of the circle and then take the last exit, before you make a complete loop, you we be on your way up Route 16 into the heart of New Hampshire and the lush lakes region.

The point here being three New England states all connect at this one spot. Approximately hundred yards from the circle itself was then located a Howard Johnson's restaurant/motel which offered several function rooms. It was one of these Ralph had rented to hold his first (and New Hampshire's) comic convention.

CHAPTER FIVE

THE FIRST HOWARD JOHNSON CONVENTION

To say I was a bit anxious when the day of the Howard Johnson con came around would be a gross understatement. I honestly had no idea what I was going to do there. I arrived early, found the hall and Ralph pointed me to the table I'd been assigned. I'd brought a thick black artist portfolio in which I kept my original art pieces and began placing them on the table.

As I was doing this, several other vendors who sold comics in various venues began arriving. A few I was familiar with and we exchanged hellos. Then the big "guest" showed up and as it turned out, Ralph had put us side by side. Joe Blowhard and I shook hands and I told him I had been collecting his comic series and enjoyed them a great deal. He was happy to hear that and both of us started up a friendly conversation as to how the day would turn out.

By the time Ralph opened the main doors and the fans started filing in, everything on our end was ready. Gradually people I knew either from town or the Flea Market started coming over to my table to see what I'd brought and talk about my recent Charlton success.

Over to my right, Joe was meeting fans and selling lots of his comic magazines. It appeared both of us were having a good day after all.

There weren't a whole many things from that day that I remember, as what I just described was pretty much how things went for the most part. The one exception was the afternoon incident wherein two young men approached Joe Blowhard's table carrying a massive portfolio and asked if he would be willing to look at their artwork and critique it.

At that my own ears perked up and doing my best not to be overly nosey, I was in fact listening to what was transpiring only a few feet from me.

Joe agreed to look at the duo's work and they hastily opened up that massive portfolio and carefully laid out stacks of pages before him. Now some of these were simply sketches of characters while others were actual, full size comic pages. As Joe glanced at these, he asked who did what. It seemed the pair were both writers and artists and during the process of creating their comics would trade off jobs. One would pencil one time and the other ink and letter, whereas on another page they would swap roles. Which was pretty remarkable in itself as from what I could see from my chair, most of the art looked uniform throughout. However they did it, they had achieved a commonality that was truly remarkable.

I remember much of the stuff looking rough and crude, but filled with energy. Most of what they were showing off featured anthropomorphic characters, i.e. humanoid animal characters. Some were dressed up like people and shown in beautiful rendered action sequences. The young artists told Joe their primary influences were Jack Kirby and Japanese manga comics. After hearing this, it was easy to see those influences in their many pages.

What caught me completely by surprise was Joe Blowhard's reaction to their work. Instead of offering them a positive critique; one in which he would both point out their strengths and weaknesses and offer suggestions to improve, he instead proceeded to tear them apart. He told them flat out that their stuff was crude, amateurish and would never have any real commercial value.

And all the while they both stood there politely listening to his vicious comments and never once bothered to argue or defend themselves. Meanwhile witnessing all this, I was flabbergasted. After ten minutes of this uncalled for beatdown, Joe Blowhard was done and the boys politely thanked him for his time… and critiques; bundled up their artwork and walked away.

I distinctly remember coming home that night and telling Valerie how cruel and insensitive this Blowhard fellow was and how sorry I felt for the two local guys. I doubted seriously we'd ever see them try this again. At that time my best guess would have been that they went back to their jobs at the pizza restaurant and gave up their dreams of being comic book creators.

Oh, their names; Kevin Eastman and Peter Laird.

CHAPTER SIX

CHARLTON COMES KNOCKING

What with our success with the Charlton Bullseye, Gary and I continued to work on various projects separately. The last thing we expected was to get a letter from Assistant Editor Bill Pearson asking us for another strip. Apparently he and Editor Wildman had been that impressed with "Duel In The Stars" that they wanted more from the newly hatched comic team of Fortier & Kato.

Of course we were only too happy to oblige them. The thing was, upon getting Pearson's offer, I realized just how magnanimous Gary had been in accepting my script without any hesitation at all. Thus if we were going to produce a second strip together it was only fair to me that Gary should have some input as to what that strip would be about, so I called him.

Understand that in those days a long-distance call from New Hampshire to Hawaii wasn't cheap. Still this was important enough to be worth the price. Gary was pleasantly surprised when picking up the receiver and hearing it was me on the line. After explaining why it was I was calling, I asked him the crucial question.

"So what it is you want to do next?"

He may have taken a few seconds to answer but not that much more. It was as if he'd been waiting for that question a long, long time.

"Gee, Ron, I'd like to do a comedy super-hero. You know, with the ability to break apart like a jigsaw puzzle and then put himself back together again."

It was the last thing I had wanted to hear. Why? Because even back then, when

I'd only ever written a few things, I already understood that in the world of storytelling nothing is more difficult to pull off than comedy. Action and adventure are run-of-the-mill stuff for comics as are fantasy and horror. Whereas comedy is very much like walking a literary tightrope in that you want your readers to laugh with your hero as opposed to laughing *at* him. If we were going to do a comedy super-hero, the odds were fifty-fifty we could create something endearing or something totally silly and stupid.

Now all of that ran through my thoughts the moment Gary told me his idea. Then as soon as they did, another followed immediately. I instantly recalled how the great silent film actor Lon Chaney had been dubbed "The Man of a Thousand Faces." The leap in my brain followed suit.

"Mr. Jigsaw, Man of a Thousand Parts," I blurted out.

"Yeah, that's it. Exactly."

Of course I had absolutely no idea on just how I could ever pull it off but I didn't tell Gary that. Rather I told him I'd get started on it right away and would hopefully have a script off to him in a week or so. We said goodbye to each other and hung up.

I felt liked I'd just jumped off a cliff. How the hell could I come up with a character who broke apart into thousands of pieces and make him work so that comic readers would like him? That was the challenge and for the next few days it was the upper-most thing on my mind.

How do you make a character sympathetic and funny at the same? Answer, make him terribly naïve without a mean bone in his body. At least that was my thinking when I came up with one Charlie Grant, a 19 year-old high school graduate from Lewiston, Maine, who grew up with this bizarre break-apart ability. You see, Charlie had two loving parents who never made an issue of his "gift" but rather supported him in everything he did. Realizing he was different because of this "gift," Charlie found his purpose in comic books.

You see our character would live in a world where super-heroes actually existed and he would have grown up reading their adventures in comic books. His favorite being Captain Justice. Then upon graduating from high school he packs his bags and starts hitch-hiking to Boston where he is going to begin his career as a bona fide super-hero. And his parents happily go along with this madcap scheme.

Stay with me people, I was clearly venturing into unknown waters with Mr. Jigsaw. All the while this wacky origin was taking shape in my imagination I kept telling myself, "Keep it light and innocent with lots of action." It would be obvious to the readers that Charlie was way too immature to take on the career he aspired to. No, there would have to be some period of training and certainly not in Boston. And there was no way he could do this by himself. He would need a friend, an ally, a mentor. Someone slightly older and lots more mature.

Enter Amy "Buck" Boucher, star reporter for the Portland Press Herald.

The inspiration for Amy came from my cousin Gloria Richer. As a child, she suffered a horrible accident which took one of her hands. Her parents refused to allow this handicap to define her and did not raise her any different than her younger sister, Ruth. Thus Gloria grew up with a prosthetic hook. She excelled in school, went on to college and is one of the most successful women I know today.

Somehow my subconscious took Gloria's true experience and wove it into my story in a truly ironic fashion. Amy Boucher, nicknamed Buck by her colleagues on the newspaper, would have only one hand and prosthetic hook on the other arm. Thus a naïve super-hero who could manipulate all the parts of his body would end by being befriended by an amazing young woman—with a part missing.

And so I wrote the twelve page "Mr. Jigsaw, Man of a Thousand Parts" which gives us Charlie's origin from his birth to his encounter with Amy Boucher. At the end, she convinces Charlie he's not ready for big-time Boston and convinces him to return with her to Porltand. At that time it was always intended to be a stand alone one-shot.

When Gary received the script, he loved it and went on to draw it near perfection. Every single page of this strip was an artistic gem. By the time Bill Pearson received it at Charlton, all the lights were green; full speed ahead.

Or so we thought.

You see, before our Mr. Jigsaw tale could be slotted into another issue of the Charlton Bullseye, that program was canceled. To this day I've never been quite sure why. Apparently their experiment failed and the book was seen as an expense they could not afford. Top management gave Editor Wilman the order to send back all the strips that had yet to be published. The Charlton Bullseye was dead.

That should have also meant so was our Mr. Jigsaw story. Instead Gary and I both received letters from Pearson in which he explained Bullseye's demise and then added our strip was one of a few he and Wildman still wanted to use. Thus they would publish Mr. Jigsaw in a forthcoming issue of their title *Scary Tales*. Note, by this time, most of these anthology series were only reprinting previously published stories. Charlton was in an economic bind and trying to get by as cheaply as they could.

Still, these guys were so taken with Jiggy (the nickname our loveable hero would eventually earn) that they decided to give him the cover spot and asked Gary to come up with the appropriate image. Thus several months later, Scary Tales # 38 dated 1982, hit the comic shops.

The cover had Jiggy battling several escaped convicts in his own unique way. The first story on the inside was a reprint of *Night of the Mummy* with art by Pat Boyette. The second was a reprint of *Satan is Free* with art by Steve Ditko. And then came our Mr. Jigsaw adventure.

The issue was distributed across the country to include a comic shop in Ohio owned and operated by Tony Isabella. (You'll remember that name from earlier.) Tony, like most such owners regularly read the new titles. After discovering Mr. Jigsaw in that issue of Scary Tales, he then picked up the phone and called his good friend, CBG editor and reviewer, Don Thompson. Tony told Don about this fun new character he'd just found in the new Scary Tales and urged him to check him out.

A few weeks later, I'm flipping through my issue of CBG and upon going to Don's review column was stunned to see the cover of Scary Tales # 38 reprinted there. It was among the half dozen titles Don was reviewing that week. In his review, Don enthusiastic applauded our strip, both in art and story. To this day I still remember how he concluded his review, telling his readers that Mr. Jigsaw reminded him "…of C.C. Beck's original Captain Marvel."

To this day, it is one of most gracious comments I've ever been given.

Later, in CBG's last issue of 1982, Don once again referred to Jiggy, listing it as one of the top twenty comic tales of the year.

Wow!! Just wow!

CHAPTER SEVEN

THE SECOND HOWARD JOHNSON CONVENTION

With two of our strips having been published at Charlton, Gary and I were not about to sit on our backsides and wait for the offers to keep rolling in. Both of us were aware enough of the industry to know that now that we had our foot in the door, it was all important we keep pushing that opening wider and wider. That could only be done by producing more comics.

Thus it was around this time that I came up with the idea of a high school English teacher trained in the martial arts who was fed up with seeing so many of his students getting hooked on drugs. Wanting to fight back, he takes on the identity of a battling vigilante and called himself Street-Fighter. When I pitched it to Gary, he was immediately on board and I quickly started creating characters and working on the first few scripts.

A few years had passed since that first Howard Johnson one-day convention though I really wasn't paying much attention to any of that. Then one Sunday, while at the Flea-Market picking my comics, Ralph announces he's in the process of putting on a second convention and at the same place as the first; the Portsmouth Traffic Circle Howard Johnson.

All of us regulars were delighted and with each passing week he continued to fill us in on his plans for the new event.

"You know those two young guys, Eastman and Laird?" he asked me one Sunday.

"Sure, the guys who work at that pizza place in Dover. They were at the last con and showed Blowhard their stuff."

"That's them," he confirmed. "They've borrowed money from one of their uncles and are going to print up their own comic book and have it debut at our show."

My first reaction was being pleased they hadn't let Blowhard's negative comments deter them from moving ahead with their plans.

"So any idea what it's about, Ralph?"

"Oh, it's something kooky. According to what little I've picked up from them, it's going to be a black and white book and feature a group of turtles who do kung-fu."

"Huh!" I had to admit, it sounded like the wackiest idea I'd ever heard.

"Wait a second," Ralph held up a finger. "I remember now. It's 'Teenage Mutant Ninja Turtles.'"

Now that's a mouthful, I thought. It sure seemed like these guys were covering all their bases. Only time would tell.

⊕⊕⊕

The next few months seemed to fly by quickly and just like that we were all back at the Howard Johnson setting up our respective tables. Once again I was placed next to returning guest Joe Blowhard. I had a few issues of Scary Tales #38 to display while Blowhard had several new issues of his mag, "The Abandoned" plus a few more pin-up prints. Whereas this time Ralph had set up the two pizza guys, Eastman and Laird at the far end of the hall and given them three tables.

I remember getting my own table ready and glancing in their direction. It seemed like once there, they were unpacking not only lots and lots of copies of their new, amateur comic but also prints and even tee-shirts with those turtle heroes on them. Now that was a gutsy move on their part. There were no guarantees anyone would even like their comic, let alone dig out more cash for tees and prints.

Thing is, as the show officially got started and families started coming through the main doorway, the little kids all seemed to be make a bee-line right to Eastman and Laird's tables. Within minutes they had a line forming down the center of the hall as the little rug-rats couldn't wait to put their fingers on this new, locally produced comic book.

INTERIM ASIDE

The phenomenon I witnessed happening before my eyes was something I would dwell upon in the days, weeks and months ahead. Eventually I would come to a rather intriguing conclusion I didn't perceive at the time. You see, ever since the 60s and the advent of Marvel Comics, folks like Stan Lee had gone out of their way to push comics as something no longer just for kids. Rather than settle for the label of "funny books" as they had survived thus far, Lee, and his colleagues, truly believed the future of industry rested in convincing the public at large that comics were in fact serious literature and meant for adults.

That he succeeded was only too obvious by the mid 1980s. More and more grown-ups were devouring comics, from high school students on through to college and yes, even into adulthood. Lee and company had succeeded.

But at what cost?

The answer to that was simple enough. By the 1980s, there were almost no more comic titles meant for children. Oh sure, Disney was still pumping out their likable tried and true characters which always seem to capture each new generation of toddlers. And then you had the nearly indestructible Archie Comics and the on-going shenanigans of those crazy kids from Riverdale High.

And that was it. Really. There was nothing aimed at 7 to 10 year olds. It was as if the industry had simply forgotten a huge segment of its market audience and they just didn't care. Thus they created a void that would last for several decades.

Until two pizza-guys from Dover, N.H., brought fourth a quartet of zany, intelligent, pizza-loving, kung-fu turtles named Donatello, Raphael, Leonardo and Michelangelo to fill that void.

○○○

As the day continued, more and more kids (and adults) surrounded Eastman and Laird and eagerly purchased their comic and other items. That the two young creators were happily overwhelmed is something I will never forget.

By late afternoon I left my own table, got in that line and bought my own copy of "Teenage Mutant Ninja Turtles" #1. I even had it autographed. On walking back to my table, I flipped through its oversized pages. The art was certainly not polished but there was a real energy that seemed to explode out of the panels as the characters were put through their motions with the same panache a young Jack Kirby would have applied sixty years earlier.

When I sat down with it, Joe Blowhard asked to see it. I handed it over and he gave it a fast, cursory look. Then he handed it back to me with his verdict. "Amateurish junk. These guys can't draw and the whole talking animal thing never works. This isn't going to go anywhere."

Of course he couldn't have been more wrong. What Blowhard didn't know, nor any of the rest of us, was the fact that the Portsmouth Herald had sent a reporter to do a fluff piece on the convention. When he arrived and asked Ralph what, if

anything, was special about this particular show, Ralph told him about Eastman and Laird and their new comic book. That's what the reporter focused on when he later wrote his piece back at the office later that evening.

Now that newspaper, like hundreds across the country, subscribed to the United Press Services which meant not only would they get these kind of feature stories over their teletype machine but they too could send such out. So, it being a really slow news day in Portsmouth N.H., that writer sent out his story on the little con and a group of green comic heroes. It was picked up by thousands of papers across the land and by Monday kids everywhere from California to Michigan, Texas to Alaska were reading about the Teenage Mutant Ninja Turtles.

Of course it wasn't enough to read about them; they wanted that comic book. They wanted it bad.

Within a few weeks comic shops around the country were telling their distributors they wanted "that turtle" comic all the kids were raving about. Before a year would pass, it would become one of the most successful launches of any comic title in the history of the media. In fact, Tom Selleck even pointed out a copy of it to his nephew in an episode of Magnum P.I. that aired shortly thereafter.

As all of you already know, the Teenage Mutant Ninja Turtles went on to bigger and better things from getting published by various big outfits to being adapted to both live action films and weekly animated TV shows. Never mind the countless number of games and toys etc. etc. In very little time both Kevin Eastman and Peter Laird were millionaires several times over and to this day, their funny characters live on and are more popular then ever.

As for Joe Blowhard, he went on to obscurity. Sure, he continued to do his small time series but in the end it led nowhere. Last I'd heard, he's still doing pin-up art.

The moral of this story should be obvious to all of you by now. If in life you ever have an opportunity to critique another's work, be kind and thoughtful. There is such a thing as constructive criticism. There is no need to belittle others ever. In the end, Blowhard's ego got the best of him and karma put him in his place.

Me, I was just lucky enough to be on hand when comic history was being made. My only one regret, I should have bought another dozen copies of that book.

ADDITIONAL FACTS-

Gary and I continued to develop our idea for the Street-Fighter. Eventually a fellow from Rhode Island named Bob Palin contacted us and said he would like to publish it from his new independent company, Ocean Comics. Thus we produced a 4 issue mini-series that was published in full color.

Along about the time Ocean Comics released issue #1 of our Street-Fighter, a video gaming company called Viacom brought out a game they called Street-Fighter. Naturally we were concerned that there might be some legal complications with both of us using the same name. Never mind Gary's wonderful logo design for our comics was nearly the exact style the video guys used.

Valerie and I went to see a copyright lawyer in Concord, N.H. to see if we had any options now that the comic was on the market. Could we sue Viacom? In the end we were told ours was the basic David and Goliath story, only in this retelling the giant would win out because he had lots more money. In a court of law Viacom would simply keep the case in litigation for years on end until we were broke and had to throw in the towel. The advice we were given was to let it go. Forget about it and move on.

Which was pretty much what we did. By then all five issues had been printed and released and at that time we had no intentions of doing any more Street-Fighter comics. The one bright note in this story was that once again Don Thompson gave Gary and I a truly amazing review in the CBG. He pointed out the obvious with Gary, i.e. his art was very much in the vein of a new Steve Ditko and as for my writing, he said it reminded him of a young Stan Lee.

Aw, come on. Don was making me believe I was actually good at this stuff.

CHAPTER EIGHT

I MAKE $35

At the same time as all this (Street Fighter etc.) was going on, I was still attempting to break into other comic companies by writing short scripts. Eclipse was an outfit that published horror anthologies and it was during this time frame that I sent them a short called "Double Exposure."

The idea revolved around a photographer on assignment in Vietnam who witnesses the massacre of a Vietnamese village by a sadistic Army officer and captures the crime on film. Upon discovering he's been photographed, the villainous soldier kills the photographer and then steals his camera. Of course he destroys the incriminating film. Upon his return state-side he discovers that the camera itself is haunted and every time he looks through the viewfinder he sees the villagers being killed. It eventually drives him crazy as he cannot escape his guilt or his conscience.

Within a month of my submitting it, Eclipse sent me a check for $35 along with a note saying they would be publishing it in an issue of their series "Tales of Terror." It appeared in issue #13 dated 1987 and was illustrated by Glen Johnson. It was my first professional sale for cash and at that time a big deal to me.

I remember cashing the check, taking one dollar from the bills and framing it. Then I sat down and wrote a check for $35 and made it out to a nearby Catholic orphanage. Having been brought up in parochial schools, I'd learned many lessons on faith from those wise little nuns. One of their many sayings was, "You cannot out-give God." Meaning simply, if you live a charitable life and are generous with your talent and prosperity, God will reward you tenfold.

So here I was having just been paid for a story I wrote. A story that came from my imagination; an imagination given to me by God. And here I was asking Him to continue blessing my writing career by giving Him the first fruits of that talent via that orphanage.

Looking back at that gesture all these years later, I know it was the right to do as He has truly continued to bless me more than I ever dreamed possible.

As you are about to see.

CHAPTER NINE

POPEYE

By the time 1988 rolled around, I was writing all kinds of stories; most of which ended up in the trash can or earned rejection slips from various publishers. The road to success in the comic book biz is never a smooth one. There are lots of potholes.

Then one afternoon, out of the blue, I get a call from Bob Palin. He tells me he has just worked out a deal with King Features Syndicate, the big newspaper outfit, to do new Popeye comic books and would I like to write them. You can believe it when I tell you that offer was the furthest thing from my thoughts at that time.

"Popeye!" I exclaimed in genuine surprise. "You mean that crusty one-eyed sailor who murders the English language, fights Bluto, eats spinach to save the day and loves Olive Oil. That Popeye?"

To which Palin replied, "Yes, Ron. That Popeye. What do you say?"

What I wanted to say was "No, thanks." But I didn't. Instead I tried my best to be diplomatic about the situation. "Look, Bob, that character is almost seventy years old and he's been done to death. In the newspapers, comics and cartoons over and over again. I mean, what's new to tell? I don't think there is anything fresh I could bring to something like that."

"Well, will you at least think about it?"

"Alright. Give me a couple of days. I call you back with my decision."

"Fair enough, Ron. Thanks."

You can imagine how Valerie's reaction was an echo of my own when I told her later that night.

"So, are you going to do it?"

"Right now, I really don't know. I think I'm going to go to the library tomorrow and see what I can find on him there. Fingers crossed they'll have something."

That last bit wasn't to criticize Somersworth's town library, but rather clarify my suspicion that there would not be a whole lot of material on a cartoon character to be found there.

As it turned out, I was both right and happily wrong.

Right in that when I asked the librarian if they had any books on cartoon characters, her response was in the singular. Whereas the book she directed me to was "The Great Comic Book Heroes," by award winning cartoonist and novelist, Jules

Feiffer and it has a wonderfully informative chapter on Popeye and his creator, Elzie Crisier Segar.

Thus with pen and notebook in hand, I sat down at a long empty table with this book and began to read and take notes. What I learned in that chapter was truly remarkable.

Elsie Segar (1894-1938) initially created a daily comic strip called "Thimble Theater" and the stars were the Oyl Family of which Olive and her brother, Castor, were members. During one adventure, after the strip had been established for several years, the Oyls found themselves in need of a ship and went to a nearby sea-side marina to rent one. The boat they rented was owned by a rough and tumble, squinty-eyed sailor named Popeye and he would pilot the craft for the remainder of that adventure.

For some magical reason, readers across the country fell in love with the character and began flooding the offices of King Features with letters soon after the storyline ended. They didn't want Segar to get rid of the colorful sailor. Rather they wanted him to stick around permanently. Bowing to the wishes of both his fans and his bosses, Segar figured a way to make Popeye a regular cast member. Within a year of his appearance "Thimble Theater" simply disappeared one day to be replaced by the title, "Popeye the Sailor."

In the course of writing Popeye over the next few years, Segar did give us some biographical information on the character but it was really limited. For example, in one strip, referring to Popeye, a caption read, "He's was born in a typhoon off the coast of Santa Barbara."

A typhoon off the coast of California? You have to give the guy credit for a wild imagination. I jotted that down at the same time thinking, "Okay. So who were his parents?" Segar did give us part of that answer when he created Popeye's father, a cantankerous old seaman he christened Poop-Deck Pappy Kidd. If you were lucky enough to see the wonderful big-budget movie starring Robin Williams as Popeye (1980), then you know the plot revolved around his search for the father who had abandoned him as a babe. In this musical outing he was portrayed by the veteran actor Ray Walston. Walston had come to fame on the hit comedy series, "My Favorite Martian" which co-starred Bill Bixby.[3]

In describing Poop-Deck Pappy, Segar said "He was a contrary soul." In today's lingo, that would be a pessimist. In other words if you were to pass someone like that on the street and greet them with, "It's a lovely day, isn't it." They would most likely reply, "Yeah, but it looks like it might rain later." In other words, they always see the opposite of what actually is before them. Contrary to a fault.

Those were nuggets I could use in possibly shaping a plot. The other element that would in the end convince me to sign on was a glaring omission. In all the history Segar made up about Popeye, the one crucial piece he never revealed was the identity of his hero's mother. It was such a hole in the fabric of the character's biography, I marveled at how it had remained ignored for so many years. The most important question never answered; who was Popeye's mother?

The minute my mind began kicking that mental soccer ball around in my brain, a story began to take shape. If allowed to answer that question, then a lot

---

3   Interestingly enough Walston also played a sailor in the Broadway Musical "South Pacific." He starred as Luther Billis in the 1951 London production. He reprised that role in the 1958 film adaptation.

of other domino pins would fall one after the other in giving me something both new and fun to write.

The very next day I called Bob Palin and the second he picked up the receiver, I asked, "Can I tell his origin story?"

"Whose? Popeye's?"

"Yes. Can I tell Popeye's origin story. If I can, then I'll write the comic for you. That's my only request."

"Okay, Ron. Let me call the guy at King Features and get back to you."

"Alright. Thanks, Bob."

I truly appreciated his willingness to support what I thought would be an impossible request. Think about it. No one had ever done a complete telling of Popeye's origin from the day he was born. In all the strips, cartoons etc. he was just there; a fully formed adult. I wanted to give the world his entire story, from the day he was born—in that typhoon off the coast of Santa Barbara— through his childhood and then his formative years as a seaman.

Whereas no one had ever done it before, I assumed that was because King Features had not permitted anyone to do it.

Palin called me less than an hour later.

"They said sure, do whatever you want with the character."

At first I thought I'd misheard him and had to ask him to repeat himself.

"Ron, they are okay with you writing Popeye's origin. So if they are, so am I. Go for it."

I confess it took me several minutes to recover from the shock of learning I had been given the green light to write Popeye's origin. Eventually calming down, I listened as Palin then filled me in on other vital facts.

The comic would be twenty-four pages long. Cool. I felt comfortable with that length. It was pretty much the standard comic size back in 1988.

The artist would be Ben Dunn of Texas. I immediately recognized the name as I was a fan of Ben's work. In those days, Ben operated a truly marvelous independent comics outfit called Antarctic Press and I was a huge fan of two of their most popular titles, "Ninja High School" and "Azrael–Warrior Nun." Like Eastman and Laird, Ben also enjoyed Japanese comics (manga) and both these series were influenced by that style of artwork. According to Palin, Ben was a big Popeye fan and had immediately accepted the job when approached.

I suspected Ben would give us a really unique interpretation.

That was it. Nothing more to discuss. It was time to get writing.

What follows is the basic plot for "Borned to the Sea," the Popeye script I wrote and Ben Dunn magnificently illustrated. If you're lucky, you may still be able to find a copy on **ebay**. Note, also have a pencil and paper ready to jot down little tidbits that may one day help you win a Trivia contest.

Who was Popeye's mother? Well, it was obvious anyone married to Poop-Deck Pappy Kidd needed to be one very tough lady. Thus I created Roxanne Crusher, a former roller-derby queen known for knocking opponents completely out of the ring with a mere elbow shove.

So the comic opens with Pappy's ship caught in that typhoon while Roxie rest below in the cabin about to deliver their baby. Pappy is frantic to reach the city and get her to a hospital but the storm isn't going to let that happen. Sure enough a gigantic wave catches them broadside and plows them onto the nearby beach. Turn the page and it is the next morning and Pappy is waking up on the beach. As he lifts his head, he spies his ship on its side some fifty yards away looking like a beached whale. He has started to run to it concerned for Roxie's well being when he hears the wail of a newborn baby. Reaching the ship, he jumps up and hoists himself to the lip of the railing.

In laying out this script in my mind, I wanted to give our readers a big reveal and so planned the action to incorporate the scenes I just describe and end on the last bottom panel of page 3.

At this point, I asked Ben to give us a giant splash panel for our first look at baby Popeye. It was to be done so that we would be looking over Pappy's right shoulder as he beheld the infant held aloft by his mother's hands. Then I asked Ben to draw the most perfect, beautiful, angelic baby boy the world had ever seen.

And brother, he delivered above and beyond. That panel is a pure delight and of course the lead-in to Pappy's dialog thus setting up the joke.

Remember, he's a "contrary soul."

The first thing that comes out of his mouth upon laying eyes on his new baby boy is, "Oh, no, he's ugly!"

Thus believing that ridiculous misconception, that is what Pappy names his son; Ugly. Meaning, Popeye's actual name is….Ugly Kidd. It alone was the reason he would be jeered and taunted by school bullies once he reached that age. Not one to be pushed around, Ugly Kidd learned to fight early in life and thus he lost one eye to an opponent who got in a lucky punch.

Pappy wasn't father material, and by the time Baby Popeye was a year old, he ran back to his life on the sea. Poor Roxie wasn't cut out to be the maternal type, though she tried the best she could. When grocery shopping, she often over-stocked on whatever was on sale at the supermarket. Many times that was spinach and from a very early age, it became a staple in young Popeye's daily diet. Enough so that it fueled his amazing strength throughout his life.

All this happens in the first few pages of the comic. Eventually reaching adulthood, Ugly Kidd—aka Popeye—follows in his father's footsteps and joins the U.S. Navy and on the first ship he is assigned to meets two other sailors who will both become important players in his life's adventures; Bluto and Wimpy.

It wouldn't be fair to tell you everything that happens in the comic. That would only spoil the fun should you be lucky enough to find a copy someday in a comic shop's back issue bin. Suffice it to say, when it was published; all of us were happy with it.

Don Thompson, who was quickly becoming one of my first fans, gave it a positive review in CBG when the book hit the newsstands. He said our Popeye was certainly a different looking Popeye, but that wasn't a bad thing at all. In the end, he said we'd capture the true essence of the character and that was what really mattered.

⊕⊕⊕

About a year later, Palin came knocking on my door again to do a second Popeye and this time I signed on immediately. Whereas Ben wasn't available, Palin hired my artist pal Gary Kato to draw it. Called "Double Trouble Down Under," I set the adventure in Australia, which at the time was celebrating it's centennial as a nation. At the same time I took the opportunity to resolve an age old debate as to the name of Popeye's brutish nemesis. Was it Bluto or Brutus? My solution, there were two of them. They were twins and in the tale, one is an outlaw operating in the Australian wilderness outback. It was another fun romp with these classic cartoon characters.

Several years later Palin did a third wherein Popeye and Olive Oyl marry and had some guy named Peter David pen that one. I'm told it was a fun book.

A TRULY SAD POST NOTE -

About a month after "Borned to the Sea" was released, something happened that educated me on the darker side of comics fandom. One day a manila envelope arrived in the mail with no return address. My name and address were hand-written and I was naturally puzzled as to what was inside. Upon opening it, I looked into the cavity and saw what I thought was crumbled up confetti. Dumping a little bit onto our kitchen table, I discovered a small white card inside the shredded pieces.

On that card was written, "You will go to hell for what you did to Popeye." Then I realized that confetti was actually a copy of our comic ripped to tiny pieces. Someone out there had so despised what we had done so much as to destroy the comic and mail it to me with his passionate derogatory curse.

The lesson learned, some folks take things like comic books way-way too seriously and that is so sad.

CHAPTER TEN

THE GREEN HORNET- PART ONE

he comics work I am most associated with is my time writing The Green Hornet series for NOW Comics out of Chicago. The circuitous route fate led me along to reach that position was by no means a straight line.

It had its shares of twists and turns. The trail itself began once again with Ralph at the Newington Flea-Market in the autumn of 1988.

"We're going to have some comic creators here next Sunday," Ralph told me during one of our weekly visits to his tables at the market. "You might not want to miss that."

"Really. Who exactly?" My interest was hooked immediately.

"They're a couple of artists from Texas who have started their own company and they are touring the country visiting comic shops to promote their titles."

Okay, so that was really intriguing. I made a mental note to be there for sure the following Sunday.

Upon arriving the next week, Ralph introduced me to two gentlemen. The likable fellow with the round face, glasses and cowboy hat was artist Steve Erwin. We hit it off the second we shook hands. Sadly, I don't recall who the second person was that accompanied him on that trip; his identity long forgotten in this overly-crowded gray matter between my ears.

What I remember vividly is Steve and I sitting down behind Ralph's tables chatting away about our love our comics, our burgeoning careers and the great characters no longer being done. We talked about the loss of such titles as Tarzan and Flash Gordon and then Steve mentioned the Green Hornet. As it turned out, both of us had been fans of the short-live 60s TV series on ABC that had starred Van Williams as the Hornet and the charismatic Bruce Lee as his chauffeur/valet Kato.

Steve told me he'd been giving much thought to how much fun it would be to bring those characters back to comics in a new and updated fashion. Because of how short the TV series had been (26 half-hour episodes total) only three comics based on it had been done by Gold Key, with art by the truly talented veteran Dan Spiegle. And that was that.

Steve rambled on how it would be so cool to have a brand new Hornet and for the first time ever a female Kato, who like Lee, kicked butt. I had no problem envisioning this concept. It was obviously something that excited him greatly and I dared suggest it might be something we could work on together.

Before parting ways, Steve and I exchanged contact information and promised each other we'd stay in touch. Thus was the idea of a brand new Green Hornet comic series born from that one meeting. I wished him and his pal the best of luck with the rest of his trip and headed home.

Over the next few weeks I thought a great deal about that idea. Despite all the other things going on in my life; family, work and other projects, it was always uppermost in my mind. To do the character properly, I'd have to once again do what I'd done with the Popeye comics; research. As luck with have it, by then I'd come to know a very knowledgeable Starlog magazine contributor from nearby Massachusetts named Will Murray.

Will was an expert on the classic pulps and I reasoned he might have some familiarity with old time radio from the 1930s, where the Green Hornet had first appeared. I dropped him a letter explaining what I was trying to do and asked if he had any material that would be helpful. Within a week I received a big manila envelope in which were photocopies of two detailed articles Will had written about the Green Hornet and his equally famous ancestor, the Lone Ranger. Both proved to be invaluable and help me build a base from which I could move forward and create something new and original that Steve Erwin and I could offer the world.

But first, a short history lesson about these characters that I learned from Will Murray's excellent articles.

HERO HISTORY

The Lone Ranger radio show was born Jan. 31,1933 at Station WXYZ in Detroit, Michigan. He was invented by station owner/manager George W. Trendle and his chief writer, Fran Striker.

Together they came up with the brothers Dan and John Reid, members of a Texas Rangers outfit chasing outlaw Butch Cavendish and his gang of killers. Through mishap and treachery, the Rangers are caught in an ambush and supposedly all of them gunned down.

Hours later a sole Indian named Tonto comes upon the gruesome scene and discovers that John Reid is still alive. For the next few weeks, Tonto nurses Reid back to health. At which point, the sole survivor of the massacre, making a mask from his dead brothers' leather vest, tells his new companion to dig another grave. He will bury his true identity in that empty hole and from that day forth become the masked agent of law and order, the Lone Ranger.

Talk about a melodramatic horse-opera. Is it any wonder the show became an instant hit across the country? The Lone Ranger and Tonto overnight were the idol of boys and girls, and their parents, everywhere. Their stories were imaginative, exciting and totally heroic. The Ranger rode a pure white stallion named Silver. He used silver bullets only to wound the bad guys, vowing to never take a life. His code of justice was one to be emulated and admired.

After the show had been on the air for while, someone had the idea of introducing a kid to the cast. As the storyline went, Dan Reid's wife and son, Dan Junior, had left him and moved to St. Louis. Whereas John Reid, the Lone Ranger, regularly sent funds to his widowed sister-in-law from his silver mine, she was also privy to his role as the masked Robin Hood of the Plains and one summer allowed Dan Jr. to travel west and spend an entire week of his summer vacation with his Uncle Lone Ranger.

When this episode aired, every boy in America went ballistic. Millions of them imagined themselves as Dan Jr. and riding into adventures with the Masked Man and his Indian companion. That show was so popular that writers would have Dan Jr. appear again several more times.

I mention this because Dan Jr. is a rather important part of yet another radio saga.

What with the Lone Ranger doing so well, after three years Trendle called Striker into his office and told him it was time they came up with another hero to capture the publics imagination. Another daring vigilante who would wear a mask and fight crime beyond the reaches of the police.

Over a single weekend, Fran Striker mulled over the essential elements of what had made the Lone Ranger such a success and pondered how those same elements could be modernized. The following Monday he walked into Trendle's office and introduced his new hero concept; he called him…the Green Hornet.

ooo

Britt Reid was a crusading newspaper publisher in a large mid-American metropolis; a career he'd inherited from his father. When his beloved city slowly began to be invaded by powerful gangsters and corrupt politicians, Reid looked to the law to deal with them. When it eventually became clear they were ineffective against this new breed of sophisticated outlaws, he opted to follow in the footsteps of an illustrious ancestor and become a vigilante.

Reid assumed the disguise of the Green Hornet, aided by his loyal valet, Kato, a young martial artist and mechanical wizard he had saved from drowning while on a tour of the orient with his parents. It was Kato who would build the super-charged automobile they named the Black Beauty. The unique ploy Reid used as a crime-fighter to pose as yet another colorful crook and thereby trick his prey into believing he was one of them. This twist is what clearly set him apart from the other radio avengers of his day.

In the end, Striker's use of the Lone Ranger template was easy to recognize.

The modern day Lone Ranger is the Green Hornet.

The modern day Tonto is Kato.

The modern day Silver is the Black Beauty.

The new show debut at the station exactly three years to date of the Lone Ranger, Jan. 31, 1936. Like its predecessor, it too quickly became a huge success with listeners across the land.

The series hit the ground running and nothing was mentioned in those early episodes regarding the hero's surname. One must wonder how it was that no astute young listener ever picked up on it. Trendle and Striker wisely waited until the show was well established before they revealed their sneaky secret.

It happened like this. During one story, Britt Reid has the police commissioner in his office and they are discussing the recent crime wave in the city. The intercom on his desk buzzes and we hear his secretary, Lenore Case, announce that his father has come to see him. Britt tells her to let him in.

The audience then hears a door open, some footsteps and then Britt welcomes his father at the same time saying (and I paraphrase here) "I believe you know the Commissioner, Dad." His father acknowledges the Commissioner and then we hear that person reply, "Good to see you, Dan. How's retirement treating you?"

Dan!

Imagine you are a youngster stretched out on your living room floor listening to this show and suddenly you are told Britt Reid's father's name is Dan Reid.

Dan Reid, your mind jumps. That was the name of the Lone Ranger's nephew. Wait a minute, that means he grew up to build and run a big city newspaper. He married and he had a son he named Britt.

WHOA!!

And just like that radio listeners across America learned that the Lone Ranger

was in fact the Green Hornet's Great Uncle.
   Hi Ho, Silver indeed!

In 1940 Universal Studios made a 13 chapter serial called "The Green Hornet" and is starred Gordon Jones as Britt Reid, Key Luke as Kato, Ann Nagel as Lenore Case and Wade Boteler as reporter Mike Axford. When viewing an early scene text, Trendle thought Jones' voice was wrong and demanded the studio have his radio actor, Al Hodge, dub in the Hornet's dialog whenever Jones donned the mask. If you ever have a chance to see the serial (they are easily available on DVD) you'll catch the different voice immediately.

With the success of that first serial, Universal ramped up a sequel released in 1941 titled "The Green Hornet Strikes Again." All of the original cast returned except for Jones, who was replaced by Warren Hull. Hull was well known in the serials and among his other hero roles he played the Vigilante, Mandrake the Magician and perhaps his most famous part being that of Richard Wentworth, The Spider.

The radio program lasted until sometime in the early 1950s.

The next incarnation of these classic characters would resurface on television as I mentioned earlier. The ABC series debut Sept 9, 1966 and ended Mar. 17, 1967. Along with Van Williams and Bruce Lee in the starring roles, it co-starred Wendy Wagner as secretary Lenore Case.

It is doubtful the studio heads ever considered doing the "old" version from the radio and serials and they merely modernized the concept. The biggest difference being Britt Reid not only was a newspaper publisher but a communication mogul who also owned a television station.

But his mission was still the same, to disguise himself as a criminal to catch the bad guys. It really was a great show.

END OF HERO HISTORY

Having digested all the above in regards to exactly who this character was, it then became my challenge to write a presentation that would offer him up to a new generation. All well and good, but as I contemplated what I had learned from Will's informative articles, the more respect I had for all the people who had been involved with the character from day one. George Trendle, Fran Striker, Al Hodge, George Hayashi (voice of Kato on the radio), Gordon Jones, Warren Hull, Key Luke, Van Williams and Bruce Lee. All of them had contributed to the history of these amazing heroes in one way or another.

Somehow it felt wrong to simply wipe the blackboard clean and begin all over again. Oh sure, that's what Ben and I had done with Popeye, but again, this was something bigger. The number of creative souls attached to the Green Hornet were far too many for me to ignore.

So what if I didn't have to ignore the previous versions? What if there was a way I could incorporate all of them into one generational saga that continued throughout the years?

Along about this time, I had read a fascinating interview with British comics writer Alan Moore of "Watchmen" fame. I admired what Moore had done and in reading this particular interview discovered something rather interesting. Moore claimed that before beginning any new comics project, he would attempt to boil down the essence of what he was attempting to do into just one word. Example, "Watchmen" could easily be filtered to its nucleus core with the word... HERO.

Could I do the same thing with this Green Hornet concept I was envisioning. It came to me immediately. The way to tell my story would all revolve around one single word...FAMILY.

There wouldn't be one Green Hornet in my approach, but several and each would pass along the mask to his heir. Thus the radio/serial Hornet, Britt Reid, would pass down the mantle to the TV-Hornet, who would be Britt Reid II, and in turn he would bequeath the family's crime-fighting legacy to the new guy whom I'd yet to create.

The more I thought of this approach, the more excited I became. I was about to invent the legacy of what I then hoped would be truly amazing characters that comic fans would come to cherish. Then I put on the brakes hard. If I was going to tell the stories of the Reid family, then it would mean I also had to tell those of the Katos as well. Damn, my task had instantly doubled in size.

Having to invent the Kato legacy instantly raised a huge narrative red flag. In all the incarnations, from radio to serials to television, no one had ever bothered to give this terrific character a first name. That demanded correcting before I could consider any other aspect of my world building. I dug up a list of Japanese names and to the first Kato (of radio and serials) I gave the name Ikano. As for the Bruce Lee Kato, I thought it only fitting to name him after that radio voice actor and thus he became Hayashi Kato.

That settled, it was time to sit down and build my two family trees.

I remember sitting down on the living room floor with a lined notebook and a portable calculator and jotting down 1945, the year World War II had ended. Next to it I wrote Britt Reid and imagined how old he would be in my story. This allowed me to do subtracting and determined what year he had been born.

I did the same for his sidekick, Ikano Kato.

So now I'd have to figure out when he would get married to his secretary; when their son would be born and how old he would be in 1966 when the TV Britt comes along.

Which is when everything fell apart. It just didn't work. I needed to have each of the Hornet crime-fighting careers take place from their late twenties on to maybe their early forties before retiring. But in plugging in the years I would require for three different sets of heroes in three generations either left me with a teenage Green Hornet or a senior citizen vigilante.

I must have ripped out dozens of pages from that notepad every time I tried a different set of years. But no matter what I did, the ages of my cast simply wouldn't line up to create a viable ancestry that worked.

After many days of frustration, I put it all aside to focus on other things. I'll get to them in a few chapters. Steve Erwin and I were communicating on a regular basis and he was well aware of what I was attempting to do. He did up a couple of great sketches of how our new Green Hornet and female Kato would look. They were great. They only strengthen my resolved to solve the age dilemma I'd gotten myself into.

One night, while looking through the photocopies of the articles Will Murray had sent me, my eyes seemed to zero in on the fact that the Green Hornet was a grand-nephew of the Lone Ranger.

Nephew! The word seemed to ricochet in my thoughts. He wasn't a grandson, he was a grand-nephew. So I changed my parameters and built a lineage involving uncles and nephews?

The logic of it was the solution to my problem. Whereas the first Green Hornet couldn't quit his crime-fighting to marry and raise a family, his brother could. So I would give Britt Reid a younger brother, who in turn marries and has a son who he christens Britt Reid II. Thus while the senior Britt is still battling villainy, his name-sake is growing into a healthy, intelligent man and would reach the perfect age to take over the family business when the original Hornet retired.

It worked beautifully, so much so that I merely duplicated it a second time. I imagined Britt II (Van Williams) also had an older brother who in turned married and had two sons. The youngest of these would become our new Green Hornet, Paul Reid. It was Paul who would then team up with Hayashi's baby sister, Mishi Kato; the first ever female Kato.

For the next few weeks I slavishly built both those family trees until they were filled with some truly wonderful characters. And in the process I committed the most rookie writing mistake of them all. I wrote a series presentation package that was over forty pages long.

Being still fairly new to this game, I didn't know that most editors and publishers much preferred short, concise presentations of only a few detailed pages. Here I was having put together what looked liked a small telephone book. I really had no clue what I was getting myself into.

I am not going to elaborate any further on that presentation or the two family trees I whipped up. The trees would be later printed in the back of several comic collections and if you are lucky enough, maybe you can still hunt them down.

STRONG RECOMMENDATIONS·

"The Green Hornet—A History of Radio, Motion Pictures, Comics and Television," by Martin Gram and Terry Salmonson— 816 pgs, published Mar. 2010 is easily the most comprehensive history of the character ever published. Whereas "Let's Roll, Kato": A Guide to TV's Green Hornet by Billie Rae Bates — 482 pgs Mar. 2017 focuses wonderfully on the television series. Both are must haves for any true Green Hornet fan.

CHAPTER ELEVEN

A FEW FRIENDS ALONG THE WAY

I spoke earlier about the advent of Comic Shops and how they quickly began to pop up all over the country. With this increase in outlets for a specific product, it was only logical more comic companies would come along to provide even more comics to sell. The decade between 1985 and 1995 saw an explosion of new outfits and new titles.

None of these new publishers were as big as DC or Marvel, but several aspired to those production heights. Chief among these were Dark Horse, First Comics, NOW Comics, and Malibu. Among the smaller outfits you had Moonstone, Comico, Eclipse, Eternity, Blackthorne and so many others I've forgotten over time.

The proliferation of new comic titles demanded new writers and artists and believe me, there was no shortage of those. It seemed like every week I was finding a new comic to read by people I'd never heard of before. Whenever I found a book I liked a great deal, I'd write the creators via their editors and thus over a period of several years began friendships with quite a few amazing people. Many of them I still keep in touch with.

Writer Martin Powell caught my attention with his Sherlock Holmes "Scarlet in Gaslight" illustrated by Seppo Makinen. Powell was big into monster comics and his adaptation of Frankenstein is one of the best illustrated version of that classic ever done.

Also working for Malibu was Steve Bennett, a knowledgeable comic book fan who loved Japanese anime. Steve produced a dystopian series about a group of young boys living in a post apocalyptic America called The Rovers. It was great fun.

Eternity knocked out a risqué series in the same vain as The Rovers but featuring a sexy woman lead character named Scimidar. It was written by one R.A. Jones and drawn to perfection by a guy named Rob Davis. I began a correspondence with Rob and when he eventually ended up working on Star Trek for DC, the two of us tried to put together a series proposal for them. Sadly it was way ahead of its time socially, and they didn't bite.

At the same time I connected with another Canadian comics artist name Tom Grummett whose artwork was fantastic. He'd ultimately end up at DC as well and was known for his work on the then new Superboy series.

Folks like these and the already mentioned Gary Kato and Steve Erwin would all go on to stellar careers that lasted a relatively brief time before the comics expansion bubble finally collapsed under its own weight.

What most people had hoped was that with more publishers and comics, they could actually grow the market itself. The skewed logic being if you had more comics, you'd naturally get more readers. Any business teacher will tell you how utterly ridiculous that concept is. It is pretty much putting the cart before the horse.

You see, the market didn't grow at all. In fact, as it has been doing throughout the 60s and 70s, it continued to shrink and one by one these wonderful new comics companies disappeared. In the process they not only disappointed the remaining comics fans who were seeing their favorite titles vanish but they were also putting my friends out of work.

By the end of the 90s many had left the comics field altogether while the few who remained found themselves struggling to find new jobs.

I wanted to add this chapter to set the stage for my part in this roller-coaster decade. It would prove just as wild and wacky as all the others who lived it first hand.

CHAPTER TWELVE

RAMBO AND THE AGENT

*I*n 1972 writer David Morrell wrote a cautionary thriller called "First Blood" that told the story of a Vietnam veteran unable to cope with his return to civilian life. When put upon by a redneck sheriff, the veteran named John Rambo, reacts violently and finds himself once again in combat.

I remember finding a paperback copy of the book and enjoying it a great deal. It should be noted that Rambo dies at the end of the book; his story ultimately a tragedy.

The novel was eventually optioned for the movies and Sylvester Stallone recruited to play the hero. Stallone saw the potential for the film to be developed as a franchise with sequels and so while co-writing the script, he changed the book's ending letting Rambo go off to a federal prison rather than dying. It proved to be a very smart move. The movie came out in 1982 as "Rambo-First Blood" and was a big success.

It was followed by "First Blood Part II" in 1985 and "First Blood Part III" in 1988. I actually like all three films, but realized the character of Rambo had been diluted in the sequels to nothing more than a cartoon warrior. There was none of the anguish and suffering we'd seen in the premier outing. He'd become some kind of super soldier and although the action sequences were well handled, there was no real depth to these new entries in the saga.

When, at the start of 1988, I learned through the comic grapevine that a California-based comic outfit named Blackthorne was about to start producing a Rambo comic series, I immediately saw an opportunity to correct that erroneous portrayal. Recalling the few Green Berets I'd encountered while in Vietnam, I felt confident I could write Rambo as a genuine, believable veteran.

All I had to do was get the job.

In those days I often wrote to other writers and artists via their publishers. I'd begun doing that with fanzine creators you'll recall and it was how I managed to hook up with Gary Kato and others. It didn't matter if that person was an amateur or professionals. Publishers were always gracious enough to forward mail to their writers.

I sat down and wrote David Morrell a letter telling him how much I enjoyed his work and that I was just getting into the comics writing game. I went on to tell him of my own tour of duty in Vietnam and how I felt that experience would be beneficial in writing his character's comic adventures. I made it brief and concise and mailed it off to his publisher. My fingers were tightly crossed.

Approximately a week and a half later Morrell replied. In his letter he informed that the editor of the Blackthorne Rambo series was John Stephenson and that he had called Stephenson and told him both of my military background and my interest in the project. He ended his message telling me Stephenson was receptive to listening to my pitch and then provided me with his telephone number. He recommended I call Stephenson ASAP and signed off wishing me luck.

Hell, he'd already given me more luck than I could have dreamt possible. David Morrell had gone to bat for me. Damn. Alright then, it was time for me to step up to the plate and take my own swing. I wasted no time in calling Mr. John Stephenson.

✦✦✦

As it turned out, John Stephenson was a really congenial, open-minded editor who was very interested in what my personal "take" was on John Rambo. In our first long-distance phone call, I tried to relate to him just how incredibly intelligent and courageous the Green Berets were. They were not only highly skilled in fighting techniques, the use of weapons and combat logistics; they were linguists who could speak several languages; including those of the natives in whatever countries they operated. They were trained in psychological warfare, social interactions and superb survivalists who could be dropped behind enemy lines and live off the land for weeks on end.

To sum it up, they were fierce, loyal American warriors who never quit or accepted defeat. They were the best of the best. Alas, the public hadn't seen any of these talents displayed in the sequels but only the character's exaggerated fighting prowess. It was my hope to go back in time and give the readers Rambo's history; to step by step show how it was he became what his commanding officer, Colonel Trautman, labeled "The best damn solider I've ever seen."

Happily Stephenson was on board and I was hired. I was then given the go ahead to write a four part story arc that would pick up where the third film had closed. Rambo would be back in the states and a guest at Trautman's home in Virginia. As this was happening, we'd offer up a flashback to his youth on an Indian reservation. Then, by the second issue, military intelligence would have learned of an Arab terrorist camp operating somewhere in the vast Canadian Rockies and Rambo volunteers to go and find it.

That was the plan and within days of my conversation with Stephenson, I was busy writing those scripts.

While this was going on, Gary Kato had somehow come to the attention of Mike Friedrich of Berkeley, California. A former comics writer and editor, Mike had left his job in New York to open Star Reach, a talent agency that represented comic book writers and artists. Impressed by the projects Gary and I had done together, he recruited Gary as a client.

Then he called me and made me the same offer.

Seeing this as another step in the right direction for my career, I accepted and signed on with Star Reach. From that point on, Friedrich would receive a percentage of my pay from any writing job he had procured for me. Note, the whole Rambo project didn't fall under that umbrella as I'd acquired it on my own before hooking up with Star Reach.

By the end of Spring, I had written all four Rambo scripts and send them off to Stephenson. He was delighted with them and anxious to get them into production. By then they had hired a young new artist named Aaron Lopresti for the series. Lopresti would later go on to become a highly respected and successful artist in the business. But at that moment he was getting ready to start work on my first script.

Meanwhile, per their arrangement with Carolco, Stephenson had sent them copies of all my scripts for their approval. Since Rambo was such a hot property, they wanted hands-on control of everything connected with the franchise.

I can only imagine the shock they must have experienced when they read my first script. The Rambo in those pages was as far away from their movie cartoon hero as Inspector Clouseau is from Sherlock Holmes.

They hated it.

Or so Stephenson told me when he called to give me the bad news.

"So what are they going to do?" I asked while attempting to fully understand how badly I'd failed.

"They want me to take out all the background stuff and go straight into the action. So we're going to cut the first two scripts into one."

It, to my mind, was the dumbest idea.

Stephenson did the best he could trying to give Carolco what they wanted but truncating my scripts was never going work. Lopresti did a more than adequate job with the art and the book was published….and failed miserably. As I knew it would.

Stephenson called me shortly thereafter and gave me the news that the series was officially cancelled. Again, not his fault. This would be my first lesson in how incredibly short-sighted licensors could be. It wouldn't be the last.

Life is filled with both ups and downs. I put away those scripts and started looking around for something new to work on.

Several weeks later a postcard arrived in the mail. It was from David Morrell and read, "Sorry, kid, you wrote him too good."

ADDITIONAL FACTS:

Good writers never throw away their work; even when it has been rejected. Those four Rambo scripts remained dormant in my files for many, many years. Then about ten years ago, on a whim, I pulled them out and dusted them off. The times had changed and now American warriors were coming home from Iraq and other Middle East war zones. Over a period of a few weeks, I altered those scripts and John Rambo became Richard Lyon, a highly decorated, black Navy Seal. I tweaked the other characters and titled the project BLACK LION…and put it back in the files.

Four years ago, while a guest at a Colorado convention, I met Kevin Johnson, a newly retired, black Army Sergeant with superb drawing skills. Kevin's plans were to attend art school. When asked if he'd be interested in doing a comic project with me, he was only too eager to take it on. What I gave him was BLACK LION.

At this time issues one and two have been published and number three is in production. For the record, the narrative remains exactly as I wrote it back in 1988.

CHAPTER THIRTEEN

SAN DIEGO HERE WE COME

From the time he became my agent, Mike Friedrich constantly urged me to consider attending the San Diego Comic Con. I doubt seriously anyone reading these memories is unfamiliar with this annual event that over the years took on epic grandeur in the mind of comic fans and the public at large. In the late 80s it was the Mecca of Comicdom and all us of in the business hoped to one day make our own pilgrimage.

Still, with what little successes and setbacks I had up to this point, I wasn't all that sure such a financial expenditure would be worth it. Just because I went to the biggest comic convention in the world and had a reputable agent promoting me wasn't any guarantee I'd land any big paying jobs. It could all end up being nothing more than an expensive vacation in sunny California.

Valerie, on the other hand, was for the trip from the start. She's always been my biggest supporter and her faith in me has never wavered once. That, and the fact she does like to travel and see new places. San Diego was too much of a temptation to resist. I brought up the subject to Steve Erwin during one of our letter exchanges and he fired back that he and his wife Brenda also wanted to attend the show that August. We decided to join forces and share a hotel suite. It was all the prompting I needed and we made plans to attend the San Diego Comic Con at the end of summer.

Friedrich was delighted.

The rest of the season flew by at hyper-speed and the next thing we knew we were only a few days from flying out. While Valerie had already seen to our travel plans—reserving flights to and from Boston and hotel reservations etc.—I was left with getting myself mentally prepared to putting my best foot forward in meeting lots of editors and publishers. I'm actually an introvert. Over the last fifty years, I've learned to create an outgoing persona that I'm truly comfortable with. That wasn't the case back then and I was more than a little anxious about how I would do once we were in San Diego.

In packing, the only thing of importance I made sure to stick in the suitcase was my 40 page Green Hornet comic proposal.

We got to San Diego before Steve and Brenda and checked into our hotel which was conveniently only a block from the convention site. We waited until our friends arrived and then made plans to meet them later in the day. With that arranged, Valerie and I headed out to the Big Show.

The con was every thing I'd imagined it would be. I'd already registered via mail as a Professional and upon walking up to the main building we saw this line

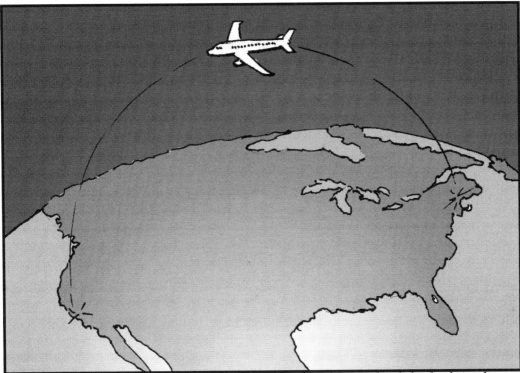

of people going on and on around the entire block. Friedrich had advised us to simply move pass them and find the table for Pro-Badges. It seemed a bit strange cutting ahead of all these eager people but others were doing it as well and we followed their lead.

Sure enough there were several tables in the center of the main reception area staffed by volunteers and a big sign labeled PRO-REGISTRATION. I stepped up to the table, gave the young lady my name and within seconds of finding it on her master sheet, she handed us our admittance badges to the 1988 San Diego Comic Con.

From there we marched into one of the big halls.

I have a vague recollection of spotting Jack Kirby walking by within the first few minutes or our arrival. I mentioned it to Valerie excitedly. Somehow it seemed appropriate that the first real comic celebrity I should recognize was none other than the man who had earned the title of King Kirby. He would be the first of many other famous creators I would see throughout the next few days. I even got to meet a few.

Our first agenda was to find Mike Friedrich. We had agreed on a place and time to hook up and sure enough there he was awaiting us. I had the sense he'd already made the circuit of the adjoining halls several times to see which editors and publishers might prove receptive to meeting his new clients.

I liked Mike from the start. He was a sincere individual who truly wanted to help his people make profitable connections that would prove beneficial to their careers. No sooner had he shaken our hands, he then whisked us along to meet various comic business characters.

One of the first such was holding down the TSR booth; they are the folks who had invented fantasy role-playing (Dungeons & Dragons) and made millions in the process. By this time, they were also into publishing books and licensing some of their fantasy games to various comic companies. Thus we met Jeff Butler, a youthful, sturdy guy who looked liked he'd just walked off a college football field. He had already made a name for himself by being the artist on one of the hottest comics out there, *BADGER*, along with writer Mike Baron. From that he went on to become TSR's Art Director which was no small feat. He was managing a group of artists renowned in the industry that included such famous painters such as Larry Elmore and Clyde Caldwell.

Jeff was very affable and to this day has one of the friendliest smiles on the planet. As it turned out he was another one of Mike's Star Reach clients. As we started chatting, Mike was called away by a passer-by leaving me, Val and Jeff to get to know each other while he dealt with this other person.

As we talked, Jeff picked up his art portfolio and began showing us his artwork. Most were pieces of the sword and fantasy genre with a few comic heroes mixed in among them. Then he turned one page and there was this sexy-pin-up brunette decked out as a female Green Hornet. I couldn't help but chuckle and mentioned my own fondness for the Hornet. To which Jeff told me he'd been a big fan of the TV series and was miffed, like many of us, that Gold Key had only done three comics based on it.

"I know," I agreed. "With that great Dan Speigle art."

Jeff's eyebrows arched, clearly impressed that I was even aware who Speigle was. "Exactly, he's one of the most underrated artist in the business."

Before departing, we exchanged business cards. At that time I had no idea just how important that one action would be.

Please understand, this all happened long, long ago and I am truthfully not one hundred percent sure of the sequence in which all these meetings occurred. Part of the time we were with Mike being led around the hall while at other times we were left on our own to explore.

In regards to the latter, the two people I was most anxious to meet were Don and Maggie Thompson. During those earlier years, as you'll recall from previous chapters, Don had been a huge supporter of my writing. I was determined to thank him personally. Happily, the CBG booth wasn't hard to find and upon seeing it we rushed over. Don and Maggie were alone at the time, so I stepped up and introduced us.

Don was shaking my hand when I said, "And this is my wife, Valerie."

"Valerie, what a beautiful name." Then he proceeded to give her a big hug, while Maggie smiled and clued me in to the fact they had a daughter named Valerie.

It was such a joy to meet the two of them. I specifically thanked Don for his wonderful review of our Popeye comic and related the incident of receiving the torn copy by the irate fan.

"Oh, I think I know who that guy is," Don chuckled. "No doubt he forgot to take his meds that day."

I think that was the one and only time we saw Don. He passed away in 1994 and his death was a blow to the entire comic world. In life we are lucky enough to have a handful of people whose kindness and generosity help us along. Don Thompson was one of those people for me. His reviews of my earliest writing efforts were the encouragement I needed to move forward and build a solid career. I was truly blessed to have known him and called him, and Maggie, my friends.

❂❂❂

While at San Diego that weekend we met so many wonderful people and I'm doing my best to recall as many as possible. The list includes Tom Grummett, Roland Mann, Jerry Ordway, William Messner-Loebs, Tim Sale, Paul Chadwick, Roy Thomas, Eric Shanower, Gary Reed and Mike Baron. There were others, but my old dusty brain has long since forgotten most of them.

I'd mentioned Mike Baron earlier when discussing *BADGER,* the book he wrote for First Comics and Jeff Butler illustrated. He also wrote one of the greatest sci-fi comics of all time, *NEXUS,* which he created along with artist Steve Rude. Within a few years of appearing on the comic scene, he won two prestigeous Eisner Awards for writing.

We came across Mike holding down the First Comics booth and maybe exchanged all of ten words between us, both of us being socially awkward in those days. Little did I realize while walking away from that first encounter that thirty years later we would become good buddies both of us living in Fort Collins, Colorado.

It really isn't easy seeing one's heroes in the flesh. One night we attended a dinner and as we stood in line to enter the dining facility, I spotted none other than Forrest J. Ackerman, or Uncle Forry, as he was known to thousands, standing several yards ahead of us in the queue. I had grown up reading Ackerman's amazing monthly magazine devoted to all things fantastic in the cinema, *Famous Monsters of Filmland.* It would be impossible to define how much that glorious magazine influenced my life.

So there he was and when I explained to Valerie exactly who this fellow was, she began urging me to go up to him and say hi. I couldn't. The thought of it simply froze me. I'd look like a bumbling, hick town fan boy. Which is exactly what I was and it would be another decade or so before I'd get my second chance to shake Uncle Forry's hand and thank him for what he had meant to me.

But that's a whole other story. Let's stick with San Diego and the most important meeting of all.

CHAPTER FOURTEEN

TERMINATOR PART ONE

Now Comics had come on the scene in the 80s, much like all the other new outfits I mentioned earlier contributing to this new comic boom. Managed by owner Tony Caputo, their business strategy was to go after movie properties and turn them into comic series much like the old Dell and Gold Key had done before them. At this time they were publishing comics based on *Ghostbusters, Fright Night, Speed Racer* and *Terminator.* The latter based on the 1994 super sci-fi blockbuster written and directed by James Cameron and starring Arnold Schwarzenegger.

It was mid-afternoon by the time Mike Friedrich led us to the NOW Comic booth and introduced us to Caputo. Here was this debonair looking gent wearing an expensive suit and tie glad-handing everyone who walked by with a voice a smooth as silk. He reminded me immediately of a snake-oil salesmen; those colorful rogues who traveled the country selling phony magic elixirs supposedly able to cure any malady known to mankind. Born in the era after the Civil War, such conmen had endured up through the time of the Great Depression. My mother actually recalled seeing a few on her neighborhood street corner when she was a little girl in the late 1920s.

I'm not saying Caputo was a conman but rather more a flamboyant showman ala the great P.T. Barnum who invented the American circus. Caputo certainly had that flair about him.

Once the introductions were over and my agent finished his spiel, Caputo began telling us he was looking for a new writer to take over their *Terminator* series. Apparently when planning the project, he had thought recruiting a bestselling science fiction author was the way to go.

That's a classic mistake many novice comic publishers and editors have made over the years. They get it into their heads that because a writer can produce over 60,000 words and get on a New York Times bestseller list, that automatically means they can write comic books. Nothing could be further from the truth as both forms of writing are as different as the sun is from the moon.

Caputo soon discovered that long after it was too late to change course. By this time NOW had already put out seven monthly issues of the comic. The eighth was in production.

"There's no action in his scripts," he told us. "Issue after issue and nothing exciting ever happens."

I listened silently. It was obvious that the writer had no clue how comics depend on fast-paced action or how to deliver such stories. What was more frustrating was the fact that the setting was that of the future as depicted in the movie. It was the wasteland where the ongoing battle between John Connors and his army battle the killer robots of Skynet to control the planet.

"I need action," Caputo all but cried. "Can you give me that?"

"I can try," I replied not at all comfortable with having been put on the spot like that.

And with that we parted company. Friedrich was all happy, acting as if I were a miner who had struck the mother lode my first time prospecting. Those were not my own feelings at all.

We went to find Steve and Brenda and have dinner.

Day One at the Con was over.

Later that night, alone in our hotel room, Valerie could sense I wasn't all that thrilled about our meeting with Caputo and his offer.

"What's wrong?" she asked. "Aren't you excited about the possibility of writing a monthly comic?"

"But I don't want to write Terminator," was my reply. "It's not why I came here. I'm not a science fiction writer."

She looked at me as if I'd just grown a second head. "What's that got to do with anything? If you want to be a professional comic book writer, then you have to write what they offer you. End of story."

Oh, I wanted to argue that point but couldn't. Valerie was right and there was no getting around it.

I'd been offered a book—a monthly that would actually pay me. And now I was acting like some spoiled prima donna who somehow had a choice in all of it. I did not. That convention hall was filled with hundreds of want-to-be writers who would jump at the opportunity being presented to me.

Thank God for Valerie. She opened my eyes and most likely saved what would have been a really short career.

The next day we went back to the NOW booth and I told Caputo that I very much wanted the job. I let him know that as soon as we got back to New Hampshire, I'd whip up several plot ideas for the next few issues and get them off to his Managing Editor.

He was delighted and we shook on it.

The rest of the Day Two was spent meeting other people. Not a whole lot happened.

Sunday morning arrived and we said our good-byes to Steve and Brenda and went to check out of the hotel. At the concierge's desk we inquired as to getting a hotel shuttle to take us to the airport. We were told one would be leaving in a half hour. Having that amount of time to kill, we decided to hurry back into the main hall and say so long to Caputo.

It never hurt to end things on a good note.

Happily he was at their booth and we informed him we were about to leave. As we chatted, somehow the conversation turned to classic heroes no longer being done in comics and I mentioned Tarzan and the Lone Ranger.

To which Caputo then said, "And what about the Green Hornet? I'd so love to get my hands on that property."

I almost fainted. Took me all of five seconds to plop my briefcase on his table, open it up and hand him my giant Green Hornet proposal that I'd been carrying around all the while we were at the con.

"What's this?"

"A proposal for a brand new Green Hornet comic series."

"Really!" He began flipping through the pages. "Looks like you did your homework, Ron. I'm going to read this when I get to Chicago. If I like it, I'll try and find out who owns the rights…"

"That information is on the last page of my proposal," I grinned. "It's an outfit called Leisure Concepts and they are headquartered in Manhattan."

He was clearly impressed. "Alright, then. Thanks. Let's see what we can do."

We shook hands, said our good-byes and off we went.

The future had begun.

CHAPTER FIFTEEN

TERMINATOR PART TWO

Soon after we returned home, NOW Comics sent me the first eight issues of the *TERMINATOR* comics. I wasted no time in reading them and as I'd expected they were a slow moving mess. The artist was one Thomas Tenney and I could only imagine how tired he must have been with drawing a futuristic war comic that was primarily talking heads.

Of course that was the relevant point the so called "author" had completely missed. This was not so much a science-fiction series as it was a war story with sci-fi trappings. Given that the movie had informed all of us that John Connor was the leader of the rebels battling the robot army of Skynet, the writer focused all his attention on Connor alone. I'm not making this up. For eight issues we have Connor running around leading his resistance fighters, giving them orders, going into the battle with them and watching many of them die.

And we are never once given any of their names!!!

What the hell?

My frustration originated in the fact that as a pre-teen I'd had the pleasure of reading DC's *OUR ARMY AT WAR* written by Robert Kanigher and illustrated by Joe Kubert. It was the ongoing story of a combat squad battling its way through Europe in World War II. There were many war comics in the late 40s and 50s, most written and produced by real veterans who had fought both in Europe and the South Pacific.

From the very first issue, Kanigher gave all his characters names from the grizzled, tough Sgt. Rock who led them to such colorful nicknamed grunts of Easy

Co. such as Ice Cream Soldier, Bulldozer, Wildman and others. Issue of after issue, we readers would follow along with them as they fought far away from home and loved ones doing their best to survive. Of course from issue to issue, there would be new men who weren't so lucky and Kanigher was never afraid to show the horrors of war; many died—on both sides.

All in all *OUR ARMY AT WAR* was an amazing comic and I can't help but believe it eventually was the inspiration for ABC's World War II weekly TV drama *COMBAT,* that premiered in 1962 and starred Vic Morrow and Rick Jason. The set up was exactly as laid out in the comic. The show lasted five seasons.

I approached writing *TERMINATOR* as if it was *OUR ARMY AT WAR* in the future and immediately defined a half-dozen of John Connor's team giving both names and specific character traits. All of this I introduced while they were locked in a bloody, all-out firefight with the killer bots and their flying death-machines. The days of Thomas Tenney drawing only talking heads were over.

I faxed the plots to the first three books I would write to the editor at NOW. She called me back and told me to hurry up start writing number nine. I was officially the new writer on *TERMINATOR.* A few days later, Valerie and I packaged that first completed script and sent it off to Chicago by Fed-Ex. We were still a few years from having the luxury of a PC and the internet.

As each issue was 24 pages long, I made a schedule by which, after I came home from the factory, I'd sit down and write five pages. Once done, I'd go about whatever chores or run what errands were required of me. Then on Friday night I'd write the last four pages, review the entire manuscript and make whatever changes were needed. Satisfied with the script, I'd then send via Fed-Ex to the editor at NOW. I always kept my weekends free.

This process worked well for me. There was no pressure in producing a new script every single week. Considering it takes the average professional graphic artist a full month to pencil a 24 to 26 page comic, I was always months ahead of the rest of the team. Writing them was fun and allowed me to create some truly fantastical challenges for John Connor and his rag-tag team of fighters.

I remember one particular issue wherein I had Billy, the youngest member of Connor's team captured by a squad of robots. They are looking for the humans' secret base and proceed to torture Billy into revealing its whereabouts. In the script, I have them cut off one of his fingers before Connors and the others can arrive and rescue him. I really thought that mutilation scene was gross.

Valerie has always been my first reader meaning she reads everything I write before I send it off. When I handed her that particular script, I was sure she was going to freak when she read it.

Twenty-five minutes later she walks into my office and says, "Cutting off Billy's finger doesn't work, Ron."

"Why, too bloody?"

"No. Just not logical at all."

"I don't understand. What do you mean?"

"Well, if Billy is refusing to talk, I'd think these robots would cut out his tongue."

Yup. My kind, gentile and loving wife actually said the above with a straight face.

"You want me to cut out his tongue?"

"It makes more sense, dear. Believe me."

As much as I found the idea repulsive, I'd learned long ago to trust Valerie's instincts in matters of storytelling. I changed the script and cut out Billy's tongue.

Now, one of the first results of that brutal action was that it totally altered the character. From that point on, writing him was a creative challenge as I, and Tenney, would have to relay his intentions silently. Not that easy a task for a writer, all the while having no dialog to fall back on. Which made me love Billy all that much more. He became a whole lot more interesting a character and he rapidly evolved into a stronger player in the series.

The following year, while back at the San Diego Con, I found myself sitting at the NOW booth signing copies of *TERMINATOR* when a young man gave me a few of his issues to autograph. As I was doing so he remarked, "I really like your writing on this series."

"Thank you," I responded.

"Especially the issue where you cut out Billy's tongue. That was so gross!"

I looked back over my shoulder to where Valerie was sitting and sure enough she had a very, *very* wicked smile on her face.

CHAPTER SIXTEEN

GREEN HORNET PART TWO

Winter arrived in New Hampshire with a freezing wind as it always has and I'd fallen into an easy routine writing the monthly *TERMINATOR*. Several months has passed since our trip to San Diego Con. One night the telephone rang. I picked it up to discover the caller was none other than Tony Caputo.

"You'll never guess where I am right now," he began mysteriously.

"No idea whatsoever," was my come back.

"Well, I'm in New York and tomorrow I have an appointment with the people at Leisure Concepts. I sent them your proposal and they liked it enough to ask me to fly out here and meet with them."

Somewhere in all that I think I forgot to breathe.

"What do you think of that?" he said.

I started breathing again. "I..I...think it's great."

"It's no guarantee yet but I will call you tomorrow night and let you know how it went. Wish me luck, kid."

"Uh—yeah—good luck."

Then he was gone and I was left trying to digest what had just happened. When

I related the news to Valerie, she was thrilled. "It's all going to happen, Ron. Just like you wanted it to."

"Let's not count our chickens before they hatch," I cautioned using a time-worn cliché.

On the inside, my stomach doing back-flips. I hadn't realize just how much I wanted to write that series until that moment. There had been other times in the past when the brass ring had come whistling at me only to zip by and elude me by mere inches. I didn't want to get my hopes up only to see them crash and burn the next day.

Somehow we made it through that night and the following day at the factory. When evening came, we ate dinner early and then I went into the living room (which doubled as my office in those days) and tried to read while eyeing the telephone every two minutes.

Somewhere around six-thirty it rang.

I ripped it off the cradle.

"Hello."

"They bought it, Ron!" Tony reported enthusiastically. "They loved your presentation and said it was different than anything anyone else had ever proposed to them."

Caputo explained that in the past two decades many other comic outfits, including DC and Marvel, had approached them with various Green Hornet presentations. All of them were carbon-copies of one another; each simply suggesting wanting to do a brand new modern version. The managers at Leisure had found my legacy approach to their liking and told Caputo this was the Green Hornet comic they were willing to license.

I do not know how long Leisure had been managing the property. What I did know was that at the time Radio Station WXYZ closed its doors forever, George W. Trendle opted to give the rights to the Lone Ranger to writer Fran Striker while he kept all the rights to the Green Hornet. Long since having passed away, those rights were then handed down to his son, George Trendle Jr. who then resided in Hawaii. It was Trendle Jr. who had hired Leisure Concept to manage his illustrations green clad hero.

So we'd done it!

Caputo's last instruction before hanging up, "Start writing issue number one!"

Valerie and I were deliriously happy. What I'd worked on for so long and sweated to make work ala those detailed family trees was all going to pay off.

"I need to call Steve," I said once the initial euphoria wore off. "He's going to flip when I tell him we're going to do the Green Hornet for NOW Comics."

Ten minutes later I had artist Steve Erwin on the phone and was telling him the good news. After I finished speaking there followed an extended silence which seemed weird.

Had he not heard me? I repeated my good news and then Steve responded.

"Ron, I can't do it."

"What? Why not?"

"Remember how I visited a bunch of publishers too while we were in San Diego?"

"Of course, why?"

"I got a call from a DC editor a few days ago. They want me to draw a monthly book for them."

"Oh."

"There's just no way I can do two. That would be impossible."

"Right." I was slowly going into shock.

"I can't pass up this DC offer. The money is too damn good."

"Of course not. Congratulations Steve."

"Thanks, Ron. Talk to you later."

It felt like I was doing the Fortier shuffle; one step forward and two steps back.

So here I was on the verge of starting a really awesome comics writing gig and just like that I'd lost my artist. Damn. Panic was about to set in but I wouldn't let it. I'd sweated blood and tears on that Green Hornet proposal package and there had to be something I could do to keep it alive.

And just like that I remembered that Butler guy; the Art Director at TSR who was a fan of the Hornet.

"You still have a card?" Valerie popped the six-million dollar question.

I raced to where my briefcase sat on the floor by my writing desk and opened it. Frantically withdrew a bunch of business cards bound together by a rubber band and began going through them.

And there it was, Jeff Butler, TSR along with his telephone number. I waved it at Valerie as if it was a winning lottery ticket before sitting back down on the couch and once again grabbing the phone.

As I dialed Jeff's number, I was mentally praying. Please God, let him say yes.

I heard the connection click and then, "Hello."

"Hi, is this Jeff Butler?"

"Yes, this is Jeff."

"Jeff, my name is Ron Fortier. I'm a comic book writer. We met at the San Diego Comic Con."

"Oh, right, I remember. What can I do for you, Ron?"

"Jeff, how would like to draw a Green Hornet comic book?"

The following day, Jeff Butler walked into the offices of TSR and gave them a two week notice that he was quitting.

It didn't hurt that Jeff was also one of Mike Friedrich's clients, a fact I'd totally forgotten the night I called him. That only made things a whole lot easier and we left it to Mike to notify Caputo that Jeff would be the artist on the Green Hornet comic and he would then represent both of us. Contracts were drawn up and signed speedily. Then it was time to get to work. I honestly don't know who was more excited, me or Jeff.

Regardless it was now all on my shoulders. It was time for me to write what I'd put forth in that mega-proposal.

I opened the first issue with an establishing shot of the Reid family mansion at night. We then move inside to see the butler, Murray, closing up the house. This was my tip of the hat to Will Murray for providing me with his marvelous articles on the Green Hornet. The butler moves to the office/library of Britt Reid where we see Reid at his desk. He's writing his memoirs on a typewriter and to the left of him on the wall above the library is a large oil painting of a masked cowboy on a white stallion.

Turning to page two we get a close up of that masked rider.

It had always been my plan to open the saga by showing the readers the connection between the Hornet and the Lone Ranger. Obviously since that western hero was copyrighted by other people, it was legally impossible for us to show a picture him; i.e. a picture clearly recognizable as that character. Jeff and I got around that by having our figure in the painting wearing a full black mask that covered his entire face thus visually setting him apart from the Lone Ranger.

Of course everyone who bought that issue knew immediately "who" that masked man was.

The panels then shift back to Reid who opens a small drawer on his desk and from it removes his own Green Hornet mask. After that he starts writing and we move in for a tight shot of the paper's heading. It read, "My Last Case."

And with that we were off to the races and I chronicled the last adventure of the original Green Hornet who had so mesmerized fans on the radio show and in those two great Universal serials. By the time I'd finished the story, it ran 35 pages long. Then I went and added a prose essay that filled another four pages for a manuscript that totaled 39 pages.

I was well aware NOW's comics were only 26 pages long. I mailed in the script and waited. A few days later the call I'd been expecting came.

"Ron," Caputo sounded irked. "You know our books are only twenty-six pages long. This thing is thirty-nine pages! What were you thinking?"

I was ready.

"Tony, this isn't just any regular comic book. We're bringing back a classic American comic hero. One who hasn't been seen in over twenty years…and all we're going to do is put out a regular comic book.

"Tony, comic fans are going to be really excited about this series and we need to make its debut something big, something spectacular. We need number one to be extra special and trust me, no matter how big this is, they will buy it. So a bigger book makes for a bigger price tag and for you, bigger profits.

"Right?"

There was a very short pause on the other end of the line.

"You really think so?"

"I sure do."

"A special. Yeah, I like that. Okay, we'll go with this."

Most people don't know that I have college degree in business. Not literature. Not writing. Business. And in that instance that degree paid for itself a hundred times over. What I'd told Caputo was honest business logic. I wasn't trying to snow the guy but rather make him see the actual sales potential this comic book would have.

Once he'd bought my argument, he in turn went out and hired one of the most popular graphic artist of all, Jim Steranko, to do the cover. Then he began advertising the book in all his other series.

When NOW's Green Hornet number one premiered, it sold through the roof and went on to become one of the best selling comics series of that time.

CHAPTER SEVENTEEN

TERMINATOR PART THREE

The remainder of 1988 flew by with me settling in to write two monthly comic series. The first week of the month I'd write a *TERMINATOR* script and the following week would be devoted to writing a *GREEN HORNET* script. All was going relatively smooth. The last two weeks of the month would be spent on developing new ideas for other comic projects that I hoped to pitch to other publishers.

One of the things I quickly learned while working on the *GREEN HORNET* was the fact that despite being about a vigilante, the book was at its core a crime comic. By that I mean every month I'd have to dream up a new criminal scheme for our hero to foil. I've often wondered what that said about my own psyche that I got very good at devising new and original crimes for my villains to instigate.

Thank God it was all for the stories. Ha.

Soon we were into 1989 and making plans to once again attend the San Diego Comic Con; which we did happily. This time we were there primarily to promote those two titles and Caputo and his crew wasted no time in scheduling us to appear at their booth on specific days and hours to autograph copies of both books.

I'd done local appearances years earlier with *STREET-FIGHTER* and *POPEYE,* but none to the extent of doing so at the biggest comic convention in the world. Lots of eager fans had lined up early before we arrived. I hurriedly took a seat, grabbed and pen and began greeting these wonderful fans. It was truly a blast and that weekend flew by.

I don't recall any other particular moments from that second trip to San Diego other than I got to talk with Gary Reed of Caliber Press again. That would prove to be advantageous a year or so later.

❸❸❸

After getting home, things went back to our established routine. They would remain that way for a few months until a new interruption to our lives popped up out of the blue.

I received a call from the NOW editor telling me to drop work on my new *TERMINATOR* script. When I asked her why, she replied that the company's contract with the film outfit that owned the rights had expired and NOW would no longer be publishing a *TERMINATOR* comic.

It wasn't the best news a writer wants to get, but then again I'd done that book for over a year and I still had the *GREEN HORNET.* So I took the news graciously and let it go. Of course I naturally assumed artist Thomas Tenney had been given the same news of the series' cancellation.

Onwards and upwards, I thought.

Twenty-four hours later everything changed again.

No lie. In less then one day, the phone was ringing and it was yet another call from the editor.

"Ron, things have changed again," she reported.

"How so?"

"Apparently our lawyers went over the contract we had with the movie people and it appears we can actually do five more issues."

Hmm, weird, but then again this was the comic book business. "Alright," was my only comment.

She continued. "Tony wants you to drop your current storyline and in those new five issues give us the final conclusion to the series. The big climatic battle between John Connors and the Terminators.

"You want me to end it all?"

"Exactly."

The wheels inside my brain started shifting into high gear. I began envisioning what such a cataclysmic confrontation would be like; winner take all. Either John Connors would manage a miracle and save mankind or it would be forever annihilated by Skynet and its killer bots. Such an Armageddon would scorch the planet.

"I got it," I declared. "We'll call the storyline *BURNING EARTH.*"

She approved. "Sounds perfect, Ron, get writing. Oh, one more thing."

"What?"

"We're going to get a new artist for this, Tenney is gone."

Ouch!

This roller coaster was starting to go a little too fast for me. It is one thing to learn you have to scrap a storyline you've invested a few months into. It's altogether another issue to learn your new scripts will be handed over to an artist you've never worked with before.

That was not happy news.

"Who is the new artist?"

"We don't know for sure yet. I'll get back to you when that is decided. NOW get busy on that first script for *BURNING EARTH.*"

It would have been truly wonderful if, where I was writing these scripts, there had been some kind of college course where I could learn all this stuff. Unfortunately most of us who learned the craft did so by doing it. One of the first things I instinctively realized about comics was they were the result of a coordinated team all working towards the same goal; making a good comic. Unlike prose writing, be it short stories, essays or novels, where the writer is the sole creator of the product, comics usually require five very different creators.

There was the writer, the penciler, the inker, the letterer and the colorist. In many instances you could add the editor as the sixth member. Lots of great comics were the direct result of an exceptional editor.

I also came to understand that it was the writer's job to know his artist and to work with him or her in establishing a solid communication channel. When I was paired with any artist for the first time, I would do my best to learn what they liked to draw and what they hated to draw. The idea was to craft a script that would suit their strengths and thus hopefully inspire their graphics.

I'd had the opportunity to see Thomas Tenney's work in those first eight issues of *TERMINATOR* before I wrote my first script for him. It was ample time to get a good feel for what Thomas liked to do with his drawing and obviously I'd been proven right.

Whereas now I was writing blind. Translation, I was about to write a script for an unknown artist; one I had no knowledge of whatsoever.

The solution to this problem was obvious. I would write very long, detailed expositions for each panel, thus providing this unknown artist with sufficient data in which to interpret the panel in his or her own unique perspective. All artists are different and no two draw alike. By writing huge blocks of exposition, I figured the mystery artist would simply edit them and leave out those elements in the image they felt weren't vital.

By the end of the week I'd written a 40 pg manuscript for what was to be a 26 pg comic book. I crossed my fingers whoever they gave the job to, he or she would prove capable of bringing the story to visual life somewhere close to how I'd imagined it while writing.

With fingers crossed, I sent it off to the editor and started planning on the script for book two.

○○○

A week and a half transpired and I get another call from the editor. They had hired the artist to do *TERMINATOR – BURNING EARTH*. He was a recent graduate from a Chicago art college and currently working for an ad agency doing storyboards. His name was Alex Ross. Obviously that suggested to me that he was a rookie and hadn't had much experience drawing comics; if any at all.

"Oh, he doesn't draw comics," I'm told by the editor. "He paints them."

Huh? I thought I'd misheard that last line and asked her to repeat it.

"Ron, he does them using markers and colored pencils and they are gorgeous."

I was having a really hard time wrapping my head around that. I'd been reading comics since a little tyke and how they were made hadn't changed in decades. Someone penciled the pages, someone else inked them, someone lettered them and someone colored them. Whereas instead of letting an inker and colorist go over his pencils, he'd do so himself with ink markers and colored pencils making him the sole artist, not counting the letterer.

The conversation continued. "He just came into the office this morning with the first three pages of your script completed. Turn on your fax machine and I'll send them to you."

Again, being pre-computer dark ages, in those days we relied heavily on those clunky printing machines hooked up to our telephones.

I ended my call with her and then turned on the machine after checking it had a full roll of print paper. Keep in mind, this wasn't an expensive machine and only gave us black and white copies.

The telephone rang several times and the fax switched on. I heard the whir of the roller as Valerie came into the room.

"What's up?"

"My editor is sending me copies of pages from the new story. They hired a new kid named Alex Ross and she says he paints his own pencils."

At that, she hurried over and stood by my side as that first sheet began spooling out of the machine. I reached under it and held it up so I could see clearly.

The first panel of the first issue of *TERMNATOR — BURNING EARTH* begins with a close up of tiny caterpillar clinging to a thin blade of grass as rain pours down on a muddy field. My intent was to show a truly dismal landscape. The next panel has a combat boot stepping in a puddle and water splashing upward.

And it was all there on that fax page. Every single detail I'd put down in the script was captured perfectly just as I'd imagined it. This kid Ross had somehow tapped directly into my vision and put it all in those first few panels. Despite the lack of color in the reproduction, I knew instantly this fellow was a talented genius.

"So, what do you think?" Valerie asked anxiously.

"Well, I know one thing's for sure," I answered smiling. "Script two is going to be a whole lot thinner."

CHAPTER EIGHTEEN

BURNING EARTH

True to my word, the remaining four scripts for *TERMINATOR – BURNING EARTH* were sparse to say the least. Those first few pages from issue number one had proven to me that Alex Ross knew how to tell a story. When I finally received copies of that first issue all colored, I also knew Ross was about to turn the comic world on its collective butt once his work reached the public.

I called Mike Friedrich ranting and raving about this amazing talent I was working with and after seeing issue one, he totally agreed with me. I even went as far as reaching out to a few of the contacts I had at DC in hopes I could make the kid some connections. Alas, I was still pretty much a newbie and most of the editors I spoke with dismissed me as yet untested with no real expertise in what was or was not great graphics.

Damn.

After having turned in the script for issue three of *BURNING EARTH*, Ross reached out and called me. He liked the idea of us introducing a female terminator and told me he had some ideas on how he would draw this deadly dame. He also had some suggestions for panel layouts and compositions. All of which I was only too happy to listen to.

Remember that bit about comics being a team effort; well I'd always work with that attitude and when a gifted artist suggested ways to make the story even better, I was on board immediately. I appreciated that first get acquainted call and from it decided this young man and I were going to be a very good team.

By the time the third issue hit the comic shops the buzz was building concerning Ross and the way he painted comics. The series was getting lots of great reviews and as its writer, I was most gratified. If this was to be my last involvement with the *TERMINATOR* franchise, then I was going out with a winner.

What I should have sensed was that things were going too well.

When Ross called me a few days later, it was with some bad news. NOW Comics had failed to pay him for the last batch of art he had turned in. I wasn't all that surprised. Remember how I said Tony Caputo was a showman? What he wasn't was a good business man. I soon learned in my short time with the company that the majority of creators who had worked for Tony had ultimately had sued him for breach of contract. (So would I eventually—let's not jump ahead here.)

"I don't know what to do?" Ross told me. "He owes me that money."

"I'm truly sorry this is happening to you, Alex. But not surprised. He's done this to lots of others already."

"So I'm being told."

"You know, you have every right to just walk away. Tell them go to hell and quit."

"You mean not finish the last two issues?"

"Yup. Alex, you're not the bad guy here."

"But that would leave you hanging, Ron. And I've got my own career to think of."

That latter part was what really worried him and I totally understood. "So you're afraid if you quit and don't finish the project, word will get around that you were unprofessional and it's all your fault the series crashed and burned."

"Exactly, Ron. I'm caught between a rock and a hard place here."

"Alex, I can't tell you what to do. That's your call. Just know this, whatever you decision you do make, I'll be with you all the way. I mean that."

"Thanks, Ron. I appreciate that a great deal. Okay, then, I guess I have some thinking to do. Talk to you later."

"Good luck, Alex."

When issue number four came out, I knew Ross had decided to complete the series.

●●●

When issue five came out, I was shocked to discover the printer had mistakenly switched two of the lettering overlays. Because of how Ross colored those pages, lettering had to be done on a clear plastic sheet put over the art. Somehow in the transfer from their offices to the printer, two sheets were switched and so the actual book had two pages in which the word balloons were inapplicable to the pictures. The words didn't match. What we had called in the army a real SNAFU.

Knowing NOW had intentions of collecting all five issues into one big package; I wasted no time in calling Caputo and informing of the lettering error. To my surprise he said it would be too costly to fix those pages and they would simply move on with putting the collection together, mistakes and all. That was it. Good-bye.

My blood pressure surely must have risen several notches after getting that cavalier response. Here was a publisher aware of a serious mistake in one of his books with absolutely no feelings of obligation to his readership to correct it. The more I thought about it, the angrier I became until I resolved to do something about it.

My solution was to write Don Thompson at the CBG and explain about the switched lettering overlays and have him print the story in his next issue ending with NOW promising to correct things for the forthcoming collection.

As expected, Don happily printed the story in CBG letting all of comicdom know what had happened. The day after that issue went out, Mike Friedrich called me.

"What the hell did you do to Tony Caputo. He just called me saying you'd gone around his back and screwed him."

I told Friedrich about the mistake and Caputo's refusal to correct it. Friedrich starting laughing. "Well, he's going to fix it now, Ron. Way to go!"

When the collected edition debuted, all the pages had the proper lettering. In looking back on the episode, I was fully aware Caputo could have easily fired me for what I did in forcing his hand. That never concerned me. I simply knew I had to do the right thing regardless of the outcome.

That was my last comic association with both *TERMINATOR* and Alex Ross. Shortly after the series was done, comics writer Kurt Busiek recruited Ross to work with him on a terrific mini-series for Marvel Comics aptly called *MARVELS*. It told the story of the arrival of superheroes in the world as seen through the eyes of a reporter from J. Jonah Jameson's The Daily Bugle.

The way Ross drew all those characters; the Fantastic Four, Spiderman, Iron-Man, Thor and all the others was incredibly life-like and so amazingly beautiful. I consider it one of the finest comic projects ever produced. And bravo to Busiek for helping showcase Ross' talent to the rest of the world. From there Ross went on to even bigger projects and successes until he was properly recognized as one of the finest artist of our times.

We finally met in person several years later when both of us were guests at a comic convention in Philadelphia. Ross came over to the table I where I was stationed and I recognized him from his pictures. We shook hands and had a very friendly ten minute chat before he returned to the people he was with.

Getting to create Popeye's mother and being the first comic writer to work with Alex Ross are two of the most memorable highlights of my career.

⊙⊙⊙

ADDITIONAL FACTS-

Many, many years later our son Alan received a phone call from a fellow he had gone to college with. This young man had gone into politics and ended up working as an aid to Governor Arnold Schwarzenegger. He remembered Alan telling him how his father (me) had once written a *TERMINATOR* comic book. He asked Alan if I would be willing to autograph a few copies and send them along so that he could surprise the Governor with them.

It was such a cool idea and I was only too happy to comply. I dug out copies from my private stash and, as requested, signed all of them. Alan had his pal's address and we mailed him the comics.

Weeks later I received a letter with a return address from Sacramento, California. So, what was that all about? I tore it open. Inside, on neatly printed stationary, was a letter from Arnold Schwarzenegger. In it he told me that when presented with my comics, he'd been pleasantly surprised. He said the comics had brought back many wonderful memories from his days as an actor. Sadly he went on to confess, his current position allowed no time for reading just for pleasure but he promised to put the comics away for later enjoyment.

Then, over the state seal was his signature in cursive and under it the words, Governor of California.

CHAPTER NINETEEN

THE BOSTON BOMBERS

With having only one monthly book to write, I realized it was my opportunity to develop new comic ideas. Something I could pitch to other companies. This being the early 90s, all those independents I'd mentioned earlier were still flourishing. The question was, what would I come up with next?

During my formative reading years in high school, aside from science fiction, I'd also discovered the master of adventure pulp fiction, Edgar Rice Burroughs. When Ace paperbacks began reprinting his Tarzan books, I took a chance and picked up a few. They were only twenty-five cents at the time.

Because of the movies, I knew the Ape Man via Johnny Weissmuller's portrayal whereby he was an illiterate caveman type with his grunts and "Me Tarzan, you Jane" dialog. What I found in the books was someone else altogether. In the original "Tarzan of the Apes" and "The Return of Tarzan," I discovered the heir to the Greystoke estate, an orphaned boy raised by Kala of the apes who, upon discovering his parents' books, taught himself to read. Later, when he returned to civilization he proves to be a veritable genius and learns a half-dozen languages. I loved those stories.

From Tarzan I graduated to Burroughs' Martian series and the swashbuckling adventures of the Confederate veteran John Carter who is magically teleported to the Red Planet and with his courage and swift sword soon wins the hand of Theja Doris, the Princess of Mars. It was as if I was in fantasy heaven and I soon learned of Burroughs contemporaries.

By the 1970s, other paperback companies got in on the act and began reprinting many of the classic pulp tales from the 30s and 40s. One of the most successful was the Conan stories by Robert E. Howard, a self-taught writer whose prose sometimes seemed to jump off the page with such energy. It didn't hurt that most of his paperback covers were the work of the brilliant painter Frank Frazetta who could bring forth mighty muscled barbarians better than anyone else.

As these reprinted pulp books caught the attention of an entire new generation of readers, publishers continued to mine those old, yellowed magazines. I began to see paperback reprints of the masked avengers ala the Shadow and the Spider. Then came the Bantam reprints of Lester Dent's fantastic Doc Savage, the Man of Bronze. One didn't need to be Sherlock Holmes to realize these colorful characters were in fact the precursors to the comic superheroes I loved so much.

What set Doc Savage apart from heroes like the Shadow and the Spider was the fact that he was both known to the public at large and that he worked with a team of experts; each skilled in a particular field.

I began to wonder what if there were another world just like ours but not exactly. What if in that world there existed a team of female adventurers renown for their globe-trotting exploits. Without fully comprehending the magnitude of the task I'd assigned myself, I began jotting down notes in a loose-leaf binder as I constructed this "other" Earth.

These were some of the key elements.

Jesus had been a woman and the Jews had fully accepted her as the promised Messiah so that after her crucifixion and resurrection, the center of Christianity was founded in Jerusalem.

As the Roman Empire grew, a full Legion was sent into Africa. There it encountered the warrior king of the Masai, Shaka Zulu. Having seen the Romans fight another tribe, Shaka Zulu saw allying himself with them would only strengthen his empire building and so they joined forces. Soon Roman soldiers were marrying Masai woman and by the time of our comic story, the South Africa in this new world is a pagan nation known as Roman Africa.

After World War One, the League of Nations built its own military force compromised of units from member countries and was able to curtail Germany's arms building preventing World War Two from ever happening. Hitler was imprisoned as a radical maniac and died in a Berlin Prison.

Without the technology developed in that war that never was, the time is the 1970s and three beautiful women travel the world as aviation barnstorming daredevils. They are the Boston Bombers and are led by Indra Devine, the daughter of the female Catholic Bishop of Boston and an Indian Maharajah. Her companions are engineering mechanic Copper Feladh of Istanbul, and aviator Violet "Rocky" Felicity of Kansas. To their adoring public, they are known as the Boston Bombers and special agents of the United Nations.

But the real secret is, Indra and her pals work for the Pope as her personal spies.

In almost fifty years of writing comics, I never once wrote one that gushed out of my imagination so fast. Once I began work on the first script, the scenes began popping up in my mind like exploding popcorn kernels. I couldn't get it down on paper fast enough. Within a few weeks I'd written the entire first saga of the Boston Bombers as a five issue comic mini-series and I was damn happy with it.

The challenge then became who would I take it to?

●◆●

Detroit's Gary Reed was one of the most innovative publishers in the comics world at that time. He had discovered writer/artist Jim O'Barr and his gothic hero creation, The Crow. Reed also gave us Caliber Presents, a truly brilliant black and white comics anthology series that impressed both fans and critics. Each issue was filled with exciting new talents and it soon became the platform all new writers and artists aspired to.

I sent Reed a letter outlining *THE BOSTON BOMBERS.*

A few days later he called me and said he was intrigued by the concept. Then he requested I send all five scripts. That caught me by surprise. Again, this being pre-computer and internet, that meant my getting those scripts copied and then packaged up and mailed to him. I told him I would have them off to him soon.

My wife suggested we take the originals to a nearby Staples and get them to do up all these copies. I agreed and then thought it would be wise to do up two sets; one for Reed and the other Mike Friedrich. Valerie agreed, though the cost to do them wouldn't be cheap.

I remember coming home with all those bundles and then putting two sets together. Valerie wrapped them up nice and neat and off to the Post Office we went.

About a week later Reed called to say he'd read the scripts and liked the story a great deal. Caliber would publish *THE BOSTON BOMBERS.* I was thrilled.

I don't exactly recall how the artist for the series was recruited, though it is most likely it was someone I suggested to Reed and he went and hired the fellow. This was a new artist as yet unknown in the business and his drawing was exceptionally clear and precise. He was very much a gifted artist and the perfect choice to bring my Bomber Girls to visual life.

After Reed and Friedrich worked out a contract, Mike called me and commented on the series, "I read the scripts, Ron. Wow, you put everything into this one, including the kitchen sink."

In looking back on my career, *THE BOSTON BOMBERS* was unique in that I'd written all of it before ever submitting it anywhere. Once Reed accepted it for Caliber, there was nothing left for me to do but sit back and wait for the comics to be published. I liked that a great deal and decided it would not be the last time I worked that way.

❂❂❂

Meanwhile *THE GREEN HORNET* continued to sell like hotcakes and fans were loving the series. Especially a millionaire from Baltimore who had made his money in construction. The gentlemen was a major Green Hornet fan and after only a few issues of series had been released, he decided to put together a two day Green Hornet event with all of us on the book as his guests along with actor Van Williams.

He called me one night, introduced himself and explained what he was going to do. The event would take place over one weekend. On Saturday it would be held in a Baltimore hotel and then on the next day, Sunday, would take place in a Washington D.C. location. It all sounded crazy and I thought he was wacko pulling some kind of joke on me. Yet the more he talked, the more I began to come around, until by the end of our conversation, I'd agreed to participate.

Hell, he was going to pay for everything anyway; travel expenses, hotel and dining fees.

The second he hung up, I immediately called Jeff and learned he'd also been called and had agreed to go as well. The construction dude was legit.

Thus a few weeks later, Jeff, inker David Mowry, myself and the entire NOW Comics staff found ourselves arriving in Baltimore on Friday night. I'd later learned from Caputo that Jim Steranko would also be joining us.

Jeff and I were sharing a room and when I found him there, we happily shook hands. Keep in mind this was only the second time we'd been together since our initial meeting back at the San Diego Con.

"I already met Van Williams," Jeff told me as I threw my backpack on the hotel bed I'd be sleeping in that night. "He's really a nice guy."

"That's great," I said. I've never met a television actor before."

Now all the while we were conversing the door was wide open and no sooner had I made my comment when Jeff spotted someone in the hall.

"Van," he called out. "Ron is here."

I turned around to see actor Van Williams coming into the room. He spotted me and put out his hand. I smiled and as we shook hands he said, "Hi, Ron, I've read your stories."

Sure you have, I thought to myself sarcastically.

"And I think you're making them a family and describing each new generation is genius. You've developed some truly amazing characters."

Somehow I kept my mouth from falling open. He was telling the truth. He had actually read our comics.

"Er…gee, thanks, Mr. Williams."

"Please, Ron, it's Van."

"Okay, thanks…Van."

"I think we're all going to have a great time here this weekend."

He was right. We did.

Time moved on, as it always does. Issues one and two of *THE BOSTON BOMBERS* appeared and Cliff Biggers, publisher of the Comic Shop News gave it a really nice review.

THE GREEN HORNET series reached the sixth issue where the lovely Mishi Kato donned the black leather and mask outfit to become the new Kato and comic fans were loving it more and more.

A comic book dealer in our area decided to put on a two day convention at a small motel in nearby Dover, N.H. and contacted me. He wanted to know if I and Jeff Butler would be his primary guests. He was willing to pay all Jeff's expenses if he agreed to attend. When Valerie heard this, she suggested we invite Jeff to be our houseguest if he decided to accept the con invitation.

Happily Jeff was on board and we began making plans.

Jeff's visit and the show went off without a hitch. The motel conference hall in which the event was held was packed both days and we signed lots and lots of comics. At one point a young boy and his sister came to our table dressed up like mini-versions of the Green Hornet and Kato. They were adorable.

There were a few other guests at this show. Among them a group from North East Maine that had formed their own little comic company. They were called Alpha Production and made up of Leni Gronros, the publisher (he and his family owned a boat supply company in the port-town of Rockland, Me.) Chris Mills, a writer who had attended the Joe Kubert School of Graphic Art in New Jersey, and amateur artists Paul Pelletier and Bob Cram Jr.

Before the weekend was over, we've exchanged contact information and they invited me to come up to Rockland and visit them in the near future. They were a likable bunch full of enthusiasm for making comics and I agreed to do that at a later date.

Jeff's weekend with us in Somersworth was a truly wonderful time for us and when he left, I wondered when would be the next time we'd get together. I had no idea just how much things would change before that happened.

Changes not for the better.

CHAPTER TWENTY

THE WAY THINGS END

It took me a total of seven issues to tell the entire legacy of all three Green Hornets and arrive at our new ones. Mishi Kato, one of the most endearing characters I've ever created made her official appearance on the last page of issue number six. After all those pages and family histories, we had finally come to the place from which we could launch ourselves into the future with these remarkable heroes.

So I'd just turned in the script for issue eight entitled "On the Pad" when my editor calls and tells me we have to get rid of the female Kato. I've never been so blindsided in all my life. Get rid of Mishi? It was the dumbest thing I'd ever heard.

"But why? We just introduced her for Pete's sake?" My blood pressure was starting to climb.

"Well apparently the folks at Leisure Concept heard from George Trendle Junior and he is very upset with our changing things."

"Huh? But Leisure read my proposal months ago. They approved it all."

"I know. But it looks like they never told Trendle about the change and he just found out. I'm sorry, Ron, but she has got to go."

It was as if I'd just been told to murder my own child and there was nothing I could do about it.

There are two ways of writing comics. The first is working for a company on properties somebody else owns. This is referred to in the industry as "Work for Hire." The second is writing material for yourself and keeping the rights to it. That is "Creator Owned" and is the keystone of all the self-publishing we see today.

The bottom line was none of these characters, even though I had created them, were mine. I had to do what I was told. Or quit.

What really got me angry was how Leisure Concepts had acted. As a holding company working for Mr. Trendle, it was their job to manage his property the way he wanted it done. They had to have known he would not accept a female Kato, but they chose to go ahead with the series anyway. In other words they did something wrong in the hopes they might get away with it.

They didn't and in the end it was Jeff and I who had to suffer the consequences.

I made several changes to script number nine, "On the Pad – Part Two" and on the last page, much to the shock of all our fans, Mishi Kato says good-bye to the Green Hornet and walks away. It was one of the most difficult scenes I ever had to write.

As if that wasn't bad enough, I then learned from Gary Reed that the artist on *THE BOSTON BOMBERS* had not turned in any artwork for issue number four of that series. After having done three beautiful issues, he simply failed to deliver anything else.

Whereas the deadline was nearing to get the book into production and meet the distributor's schedule, Reed begged me to contact the kid and see what was going on.

I tried but to no avail. All phone calls went unanswered. I sent letter after letter and still no replies. I reported back to Reed and he did his best to contact our missing guy.

It was as if the artist had simply vanished. Poof. Gone in a puff of smoke.

Ultimately the deadline came and went and Reed had no choice but to cancel the series. He hated having to do it, but he had a business to run. I never held it against him and let him know I was grateful regardless.

So you can see, it really doesn't matter what size a company is, all kinds of things can go wrong when producing comics. With *THE BOSTON BOMBERS* I was reminded of an old saying my writing colleagues often bantered around. If it wasn't for the artist, comics would be fun.

Ouch.

I'm sure artists have a similar saying about us writers.

The bottom line here, as I've eluded to before is the simple fact that making comics is a team effort and it requires everyone to do their part. All it takes is one bad player to destroy a project. It would be years before our lost artist resurfaced and working for DC no less. But we'll get to that epilogue later on.

Nearing the end of my first year on *THE GREEN HORNET* much of the fun was gone thanks to having lost Mishi. Oh, Jeff and I plodded along with issues nine through twelve. We were professionals and never once missed a deadline. We'd found other stories to tell.

About the time I turned in the script for number eleven, NOW failed to send me my check for issue number ten. I reported this to Mike Friedrich and he said he would look into it. I went on to write issue number twelve while I awaited news about what was happening.

When Friedrich finally called it was to tell me that he'd discovered NOW Comics was having serious money problems and Jeff and I were not the only creators not being paid. He sensed, from his own years in the comics field, that NOW might not be around for much longer and suggested I stop writing for them immediately.

Based on that suggestion, I notified my editor upon submitting the script for number twelve, that I wouldn't be doing any more until I received what was owed me. She didn't respond one way or another.

That being the case, I hired a lawyer to sue NOW Comics. Eventually I received the seven hundred dollars I was owed.

Issue twelve was printed and I later learned Caputo had hired Canadian writer Dave Darrigo to take over writing the series. Darrigo turned in scripts for issues thirteen and fourteen. They were never published. He was never paid.

Shortly after issue number twelve, my last script, NOW Comics filed for bankruptcy and closed its doors.

CHAPTER TWENTY-ONE

ALPHA PRODUCTIONS

With the end of NOW Comics, I once again looked to find new projects to keep my career moving forward. I'd taken Leni Gronros up on his offer to meet with the Alpha Productions crew and we all hit if off splendidly. Having no other commitments, I thought it might be fun to do a comic series with them and suggested the idea at one of our first informal meetings.

Leni loved the idea and so I came up with a science fiction story about a young Iroquois lad who is killed by a bear before he can prove himself a warrior. Because of this the Great Spirit sends his soul into the distant future where the Earth has been invaded by conquering alien races. There, a band of brave human rebels are waging a guerrilla campaign to shake off the ruling invaders and regain their freedom. One of the human scientists had stolen alien technology with which to build an artificial human cyborg equipped with all kinds of organic weaponry only to be stymied when activating the artificial super-warrior.

Which is when the Indian lad's soul enters that of the cyborg and takes over the body and thus returning to life. The Indian's name is Angara and we called the series, *TOTEM-Sign of the Wardog.* Paul Pelletier agreed to pencil it and Bob Cram Jr. was our inker/letterer. Everything was set except for one final point.

Because Alpha was such a small outfit and had no funds, other than what Gronros used to print the comics, I couldn't see myself telling Mike Friedrich that I wanted to work with this little group of creators nor have him bother them with ridiculous contracts for something that would really never make any substantial earnings. Thus I wrote the series under the penname of Scott French and Friedrich was none the wiser for it.

It was a great deal of fun for me to be with this group of young, talented and enthusiastic creators. Pelletier's work was in its infancy and though wonderful to look at, it was impossible not to see the influences of artist John Byrne. It was clear Pelletier was inspired by the Canadian-born artist. In working with the young man from Lewiston, Maine, I did my best to make him see other perspectives in interpreting scripts. I explained to him how doing a drawing the easy way wasn't always the best way. Pelletier was also extremely reticent about submitting his work to either Marvel or DC.

It was clear as time went on that he had tremendous potential and would ultimately become a professional graphic illustrator. How that eventually happened is another story I will relate in the next few chapters, I promise.

My association with Alpha lasted almost two years. Another member of the group was a really great guy names Rick Lowell who owned several comic shops in Maine at the time. During those few years, Alpha published at least four issues of TOTEM, plus a giant-sized annual. They also published a series by writer Chris Mills called *BLOODTHIRST* and several anthologies include one featuring crime stories that Mills edited entitled *NOIR.* Mills' forte was crime fiction and he was excellent at it, though he also dabbled in other genres ala superheroes and sword and sorcery.

At one point someone at Alpha had the idea that we should do an old-fashioned superhero team book and each of us contribute an original character to what we'd call Task Force Alpha. Everyone liked the idea and my contribution was Major Liberty; a female version of my favorite comic book hero, Captain American. All of us started working on new stories to feature our characters. The first book would be a giant special with a team story at the front and then several short tales of the individual characters in the back.

All the while this was going on, Mills and Gronros somehow contacted writer Nick Cuti and artist Joe Staton and convinced them to allow Alpha to do three brand new E-MAN comics. E-MAN was a character the duo had first created for the late Charlton Comics. When Charlton folded they took the property to First Comics. Alas, as I've mentioned previously, First Comics also went the way of the Dodo bird leaving this unique and fun character in limbo. Somehow the pitch the boys made worked and Nick and Staton agreed to do three new E-MAN comic adventures for Alpha Productions.

Whereas both of them, especially Staton, were extremely busy with other gigs, they could only provide stories that would only be sixteen pages long making for really small comics unless they could find back material for the books. Which was when Mills suggested Gary Kato and I do three brand new MR. JIGSAW shorts to round out the new E-MAN mini-series. I thought it was a great idea and called Gary. He was instantly aboard and soon our beloved Jiggy was back in action just like that.

I will always be grateful to the Alpha gang for this. Somehow through the passing years, Gary and I managed to keep Jiggy alive in comics.

000

With Mr. Jigsaw back in print, a few things happened in quick succession. The first was a call from Mike Friedrich telling us that a television producer had somehow tripped over a previous Mr. Jigsaw strip and thought the character would have much potential as a Saturday morning cartoon show on one of the three big networks. Naturally, we agreed.

The producer wanted to pay us $3,000 to option Mr. Jigsaw for one full calendar year. Friedrich explained that should he be able to sell the property, then he'd have rights to all the merchandising that might result. It also meant Gary and I couldn't produce anything with the character, except for the comic book, during that year.

Seeing that no one else was clamoring to get their hands on Jiggy at that time, Gary and I decided to take the cash and we signed the option.

Six months later I was called by a reporter at the Portland Press Herald who had discovered Jiggy in one of Rick Lowell's comic shops. She asked to interview me for an article about "Maine's only living super-hero" as we tagged him in the comics. Thus over the next hour she questioned me at the end of which she told me the article would appear in their big Sunday supplement.

Sure enough, the story appeared in the paper along with a reproduction of the latest book's cover and a few panels from the interior. All of us where delighted with the piece little realizing what effect it would have on local Maine comic readers. Within days of the feature appearing, kids were going into Maine comic shops looking for Mr. Jigsaw.

Two weeks later, shortly after dinner, I received a phone call from a woman in Portland telling me she represented the big retailer, J.C. Penny. She was one of their marketing managers and had seen the Mr. Jigsaw newspaper story. She and her staff thought he was such an original and funny cartoon character that they could easily promote him via a line of children's merchandising; everything from toys to backpack and bedding. If we were willing to deal with them.

Which is where I recalled the TV producer and his exclusive option rights.

I then had to tell this woman that the property was locked up and there was nothing I could do about that. She regrettably hung up and I knew fate had dealt us a cruel hand.

The producer's option time ran out and he was never able to sell a series...or anything else. Our one golden chance at the brass ring had passed us by never to return.

It was a lessoned learned. Since then I've never given up any rights to whatever I create nor will I ever do so again.

CHAPTER TWENTY-TWO

ONE MORE GREEN HORNET

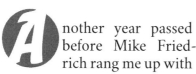

nother year passed before Mike Friedrich rang me up with some surprising news. Tony Caputo had somehow convinced a very successful textbook publisher to finance the rebirth of NOW Comics. Once that was accomplished, Caputo immediately went about reacquiring the rights to the properties they had published including the Green Hornet.

Friedrich was calling because Caputo had contacted him in regards to getting me to come back and write this new second volume. This being the same person who had tried to cheat me and then, without warning, forced me to do away with a character I had created and who was really something special to me.

It took me all of two second to tell Friedrich, "No thanks. I don't want any part of that."

In my mind, getting involved with this new version of NOW Comics would be a step backward. I needed to focus my energies on what opportunities awaited me in the future.

✪✪✪

A week later I received a call from fellow comics writer Chuck Dixon. Chuck and I had met a few years earlier at a small convention in Portland, Maine and hit it off. Back then he was primarily known for his work on Airboy, the Golden Age aviation hero from the 1940s as then being published by Eclipse Comics. I was a fan of the series and his writing skills. During that one meeting we discovered we were both Baby Boomers; our fathers having served in World War Two.

Chuck was calling to tell me he had just been approached by Caputo to write the new Green Hornet series. He was curious as to whether or not that offer had been extended to me. As it turned out, Chuck had enjoyed my stories and was leery of taking the job if it turned out Caputo hadn't first reached out to yours truly.

That's called integrity and there is very little of it in the business world. Far too many creators would stab each other in the back to land a job. This one call said a whole lot about Chuck's character and I appreciated it a great deal.

I assured him that I had been offered the assignment and that for my own personal reasons, I'd declined it. I added that I was happy that he would be the writer to take over those characters. That assured me they would be in good hands.

Chuck told me his own personal wish was to someday write the Lone Ranger; a dream he would later realized via Dynamite Comics. Along the way he would also take charge of DC's Robin series and elevate it to new heights of action and adventure.

Our conversation ended with my wishing him luck on the Green Hornet.

✪✪✪

When the new Green Hornet series debut, I bought it being curious to see how Chuck would handle the characters and in what direction he planned to take them. From the very first issue it was clear, like me, Chuck knew this was at heart a crime comic and that was how he wrote it. There were colorful villains and tons of action.

It was obvious fans were thrilled to have the Green Hornet and Kato back. What I never expected was that Caputo would come up with a silly plot gimmick to bring back Mishi Kato. In the new series, he had Chuck use her in a new guise as an independent vigilante called the Crimson Wasp. It really was a dumb idea, but hey, no longer any of my concern. Let them do whatever they wanted. I had other projects taking shape.

The one thing I did take note of was the absence of artist Jeff Butler on the new series. Apparently Jeff had also taken a pass on returning to it. That proved to be the case…but not entirely. It seemed my old partner had other plans and wasn't quite ready to show them off yet.

✪✪✪

I continued to have fun working with Alpha Productions. At one point, Leni Gronros suggested Alpha collect the four issue STREET-FIGHTER series originally published by Ocean Comics and put it out as a black and white graphic novel. It was a great idea and augmented it by offering to do a brand new short Street-Fighter story that would appear at the back of the book as a bonus feature.

When I ran it past artist Gary Kato, he laughed and told me to get writing. What I came up with was an eight page yarn called "The Wheelman." Gary not only drew it in record time, but along with the completed pages, he also did up a brand new cover for the book.

This having been the very first on-going series Gary and I had ever done together, it was a real joy to see it back in print and on the market again.

✪✪✪

At times there exist a poetic symmetry to life. When one considers that it was I who pulled Jeff Butler into the world of the Green Hornet and Kato, then it only seems right that he would be the one to cajole me back to it. All of which started with his phone call one night, months after the new comic series had begun.

Although unwilling to take on the monthly book, Jeff had this idea about the two of us doing a four issue mini-series that would feature the original character from the radio show and cliff-hanger series. It was clear when we'd originally put forth our Green Hornet, Jeff had relished drawing the 30s and 40s world; the style of clothing, the buildings and automobiles. It had been extra fun for him.

He continued to give me more details on this retro-adventure. He wanted us to give it a cliff-hanger feel. He was very much aware of my love of the serials. Ergo, as he spoke, images began to take shape in my mind. Yeah, I mused while he rambled on, each of the first three issues would end with the Hornet and Kato in a perilous situation leaving the readers to wonder how they would manage to survive…until the next issue came out.

Jeff also thought we should throw in lots of special cameos ala Captain America. What with the character owned by Marvel, we'd have to figure a clever way to make his appearance come off without infringing on those rights. But it could be done with a little bit of imagination.

"And what if they didn't use up all the Super Soldier serum?" Jeff asked getting more and more excited as we talked. "What if there were a second super agent along the lines of Steve Rogers?"

"We'll call him Lee Powell," I jumped in catching Jeff's fever. "After the Republic Pictures star who joined the Marines in World War II and died fighting in the South Pacific." The new character would be our tribute to Powell.

As you can see, that one phone call was a very animated conversation. At the end of our conversation, I told Jeff that if he could sell it to Caputo and the new editorial staff at NOW, I'd sign on to write it. But getting that done would be all on him.

He agreed happily. Before we hung up, we christened the new project.

It would be called, THE STING OF THE GREEN HORNET.

Having deduced that Caputo still wanted me and Jeff back working on the character, I wasn't the least bit surprised when the new lady editor gave Jeff the go-ahead. He then called Mike Friedrich who worked out the contracts and then called me again.

By that time I'd worked out the plot and shared it with Jeff in detail. The setting was the year before the United States' entry in World War II. Fearing what that will do, Hitler's strategists devise an insidious plot to kidnap President Franklin Roosevelt and thus demoralize the country. Led by a beautiful, but deadly female spy, a team of Nazi agents infiltrate the country. Four of them have had plastic surgery so that each resembles a powerful criminal mob boss. The lady spymaster's plan is to have the American mobs go to war against each under and thus cause all manner of chaos across the land.

In setting this up, we had Jeff draw the mob honchos to look like famous movie stars who had starred in gangland films. The included James Cagney, Humphrey Bogart and Edward G. Robinson. The fifth male spy was an exact double of President Roosevelt and would assume his place in the government once the real Roosevelt had been snatched.

By now, Jeff was practically jumping for joy on the other end of the telephone line. He loved the plot and urged me to get the first script to him as fast as was humanly possible. I did that easily enough as working with Jeff was all the motivation I needed.

We'd always been an effective team and this new project would prove to be no exception by the time it was completed.

Being a pulp enthusiast even in those days, I brought the Shadow into the story. Only we called him "The Dark Agent." When a group of dockside thugs believe Kato is a Japanese spy and attack him, he is rescued by a blond-haired G.I. who hurls a trash can lid into two of the brutes. He tells Kato his name is Steve before walking away to catch a bus.

The new super-soldier Lee Powell donned a costume and became Commando Yank. At a secret naval base, two security guards are heard talking about an underwater fish-man who has wings on his feet. And later in issue number three two very familiar newspaper reporters are seen leaving the President's special railroad car. He has dark hair and glasses and is called Clark, while his lovely brunette colleague is referred to as Lois.

Before Jeff began work on the comic pages, he did some promotional posters for NOW which they plastered inside all their other titles. They pretty much told the world that the team of Fortier & Butler was back on a very special new Green Hornet comic.

Even without that fanfare publicity, seeing Jeff's early pages, I knew we were going to give our readers something they would talk about for years to come.

I wasn't wrong.

❂❂❂

CHAPTER TWENTY-THREE

THE MADISON SHOW

As I was putting the finishing touches on STING, I learned that NOW Comics planned on having a big booth at the upcoming summer retailers show in Madison, Wisconsin. This was an annual event sponsored by Diamond Distribution and all the invited attendees were comic shop owners from around the country.

I believe it was Jeff who informed me of the show and that NOW was hoping we could attend. That simply meant they wanted us there but we'd have to pay for our own travel and accommodations. Knowing that it would be an expensive trip I initially debated whether or not to go. Then I learned that Gronros and the Alpha team were also planning to attend and that decided me. I called Gronros and told him I wanted to tag-along and he was delighted. Then I let Jeff and the NOW editorial staff know I'd be going.

Plans were made and when the weekend of the show rolled around, I drove up to the Portland, Me. airport where I hooked up with my Alpha buddies and off we went to Madison.

❂❂❂

By this time in my career, I'd been to lots of comic shows, including twice to the big San Diego shindig. Still I'd never done anything quite like the Madison exhibition. You've never seen a party until you bring together hundreds of entrepreneurs whose business is comic books.

The NOW booth was huge and they had giant posters of most of their titles, including one for the new Mr. T series they were about to launch in the Fall. Ever the showman, Caputo also had Mr. T himself on hand to help promote the comic and meet the fans. Knowing of his military background before going into acting, I managed to get a picture of the two of us shaking hands and had him autograph it for our son Alan, who at that time was in basic training. Mr. T was as charming and affable as he appeared in the hit TV series, THE A-TEAM.

When Jeff arrived, the new editor had now introduced herself to us, then ushered us to our chairs. They had set up several long tables in a line with me and Jeff situated at the last one. As people came to the booth, they first encountered members of the editorial staff who gave them several Green Hornet posters showcasing STING and then these enthusiastic folks would have me sign them before handing them off to Jeff to do likewise.

We began this process at 10:00 a.m. and would not stop until six that evening. Nobody bothered with keep an accurate count, but it would be a safe estimation to say during the course of that one day, we signed well over three hundred comics and posters; if not more. Again, do keep in mind, all these people we met were all owners of comic shops and they were so kind to us. Many of them told us how much they had loved our run on the first Green Hornet volume and how successful the comic had been with their customers. Ergo, they were most anxious for the release of STING.

After signing the posters of a husband and wife couple, I was surprised when he handed me a square white wall tile. He explained that they were in the process of redecorating their shop and he wanted to cover an entire wall with the signatures of comic book writers and artists. Thus he brought lots of these white tiles to the show. I grabbed a black sharpie and put my name on it. The fellow had one for Jeff as well.

Over the years I've signed lots of things including the dashboard of a beautiful custom made Black Beauty automobile.

As the day wore on, I kept signing my name over and over and over again. So much so that at one point, I took a second to flex the muscles in my right hand. Then when I reached for the next poster to autograph, I had a brain freeze. Jeff sensed my hesitancy and looked at me puzzled.

"What's wrong, Ron?"

I looked at him and shook my head. "I just forgot how to write my name for a second."

We laughed. He understood completely. I cleared the cobwebs out of my head, and got back to writing. Everything being back to normal.

○○○

As the afternoon began to wind down, the NOW editor, who had been seated to my left all day, leaned over and hit me with the last question I ever expected to hear. "How would you like to come back and write the regular monthly?"

Surprised, I looked at her to see if she was joking. She wasn't.

"What happened to Chuck Dixon?" I queried while still signing posters.

"He just notified us a few days ago that he's got other commitments and is all done after issue five."

I didn't know what to say to that. Up to this point I'd been content with my decision not to return to that series. Yet here I was promoting the STING mini-series, having a fun time and all too aware taking on the job would help our finances.

That and I actually missed that cast of characters Jeff and I had created and developed.

At that point, I turned to Jeff and repeated what I'd just been offered. Would he have any interest in being a part of that? Sadly he was adamant about calling it quits after he wrapped up his work on STING. If I took the gig, it would be on my own. I'd have to work with other artists.

In looking back on it, the temptation was too great to resist and I told Ms. Editor to tell Caputo to draw up the contracts.

I was back on the Green Hornet.

○○○

Caputo's luck with the second incarnation of NOW Comics wouldn't fare any better than the first. Regardless of how many gimmicks they came up with, the company's revival wouldn't last more than a year. What I recall from that period is vague and I find myself actually looking through those issues that I did write to refresh my memory.

One experience does stick out above all the others and that was how I was tasked into writing the origin of Mishi's new persona; the Crimson Wasp. No sooner had I returned home from the Madison seminar than Ms. Editor called me to explain their plan for the character. They wanted a story that would take three issues to tell under the banner of "The Odyssey of the Crimson Wasp."

None of that was a problem until she told me she wanted all three scripts on her desk within a week. I told her that was impossible. At which point she elaborated on their strategy to make it happen. I was to write out a loose plot outline for each of the three issues and send them in. Then while I was writing chapter one, they would have another writer doing chapter two from my outline. She told me who they had in mind to recruit. With both those turned in simultaneously to two different artists, I'd wrap it all up by writing the third and final chapter.

Although she did her best to convince me it would work, I saw too many ways it could all fall apart. I knew of this other writer she had named and wasn't at all impressed by his credentials. In fact most of his work I'd read was dull and boring. There was no way I wanted to let him be any part of this narrative.

I had to come up with an alternative. Here it was mid-week and she wanted all three scripts on her desk by the following Monday.

"I'll write them all," I blurted, stalling any further debate from her.

"By next Monday?"

"I'll have it done by Monday. You'll have it on your desk by Tuesday. You have my word. This can only work if I write the entire story-line."

She reluctantly gave in and as I broke the connection, I wondered just what the hell I'd gotten myself into.

I spent the next two days working out a plot that would logically explain what had happened to Mishi after she had left the first series and the tragedy that befell her shortly thereafter. Several people she had come to love had been brutally murdered and she was left for dead. Upon her recovery she vows vengeance against the villain and transforms herself into a modern day female samurai, aka the Crimson Wasp.

With the basic plot developed, my next step was setting up exactly how I would achieve my goal of writing all three over a one week-end period. I told Valerie and she agreed to do whatever was needed.

The following day, a Thursday, I went to my boss at G.E. and told him I would not be in the following day; taking use of a personal day I had accrued. That taken care of, all that was required now was to do the actual writing.

Friday morning came, I had breakfast, then with a second cup of coffee, went to my desk and began writing script #1. Valerie interrupted me for lunch and after eating, I was back at it. I never stopped until dinner. The story was nearly done.

By 7 p.m. that evening I finished page #24 with "….to be continued." I printed out the script and stuck in a manila enveloped. I watched a little TV and then went to bed.

Saturday morning I was up early, ate a small breakfast and then went back to it. As the day wore on, the story began to take a life of its own as I wrote page after page propelling Mishi Kato along the most hazardous, obsessive challenge of her life.

By 9 p.m. chapter two was completed. I was two/thirds done.

Sunday was a repetition of Friday and Saturday with me glued to my desk pounding away at the third and climatic chapter in the adventure. With most of the story's elements having been established in the first two chapters, all that remained was the final confrontation with Mishi's foe. In the big end battle, the Green Hornet and Kato enter the fray to fight at her side. The Crimson Wasp is victorious and with that I happily slapped THE END on the last page.

Sitting there at my desk, I stacked all three scripts atop each other. I had written 72 comic pages in just three days. There was a tremendous sense of joy and accomplishment for sure. But when I sent it off via Fed-Ex next day delivery, I promised myself I would never do that again.

It was nuts.

⊕⊕⊕

During that run, I created a few interesting characters ala Sister-Hood and Mr. Death and worked with a variety of talented artists. In issue # 21, "The Return of Mr. Death" was drawn by a new kid from South America named Joe Bennett. It was his first ever professional comics work and today he's one of the finest artists in the business, working for both Marvel and DC and always in demand.

Other artists who I enjoyed teaming with were Zal Veluto and Patrick Zircher. I remained with the series until issue # 28. By then rumors had started circulating that NOW was once again in financial trouble and my last two scripts had gone unpaid. I remember calling the editor and telling her that I was through.

That she didn't seem surprised only confirmed my suspicions. Within a few months, NOW Comics went under for a second and final time.

It's really a sad tale. Had Caputo had any real business know-how, he might have kept it alive. But that's a big what if. The truth is, while it lasted, NOW Comics offered a mix of products; some good, some mediocre. What it did do was give many young creators an opportunity to break into the comics world.

I was one of those and for that I will always be grateful. To this day, regardless of what other projects I've worked on, people still connect me with the Green Hornet.

Not a bad reputation at all.

CHAPTER TWENTY-FOUR

PETER PAN

Malibu Comics was a terrific outfit born in the 80s boom and at its head were three men, David Olbrich, Chris Ulm and Tom Mason. They produced many great comic series and I enjoyed their comics very much. Enough to hope that some day I could write something for them.

That eventually happened, but only after they had created a subsidiary line they called Adventure Comics and the project I sold them was a two part Peter Pan adventure.

From the first time I saw Walt Disney's animated version of the James Barrie children's classic, I fell in love with it. The concept of a place where kids would never grow up and live every day having daring adventures was just too perfect for my young imagination. As I grew older, I read Barrie's book and my admiration for the story grew. Once I'd established myself as a professional comic writer, I thought it time to relive my own daydreams of Never-Never Land in a brand new tale of Peter and his Lost Boys.

Almost like BOSTON BOMBERS, I simply sat down one day and wrote a two part script entitled "Return to Never-Land." In it Peter Pan comes to Roxbury Massachusetts in search of American cowboys. Obviously this is a fantasy and poor Peter had no concept of the American west. Whereas the whims of fate intervene and he stumbles upon two young brothers who happened to love cowboy movies and are always wearing their cowboy hats, vests and toy-pistols.

Not knowing any better, Peter, whisks them away to Never-Never Land to help him capture old discarded carousel horses that actually come alive on the magic island. The problem is the paint on these wooden horses is worn and peeling away. It's Peter's wish to capture them and repaint them so that they will look brand new. Then he and his Lost Boys can have fun riding them. Unfortunately the animals prove nearly impossible to capture and so that is why Peter comes to America; to find cowboys.

I wrote a 48 page story in two parts, each 24 pages long. Then I reached out to my buddy Gary Kato and asked if he would like to draw it should I be able to sell it. Gary loved the concept, did up a few sample sketches of Peter and sent them back to me. I added these to my presentation package and sent it off to Adventure Comics.

Their response was sooner than I'd expected and much to my delight, they did want the project. They also decided to print it in full color. I connected them with Gary and within months issue number one was in comic shops everywhere. It was by far the fastest project I'd ever had turned around. Gary's artwork was simply sensational and Cliff Biggers of the Comic Shop News gave it a most positive review. The following month, right on time, issue number two arrived. Then, to my total and happy surprise, a few months later, Adventure Comics did a third collected edition as a special one shot.

Like most of the comics I've written, I have a few of these Peter Pan issues stashed away for safe keeping. Every now and then, when I look at them, I'm still happy with how the project all worked out.

One little-known fact is the special cameos that appear in the story. You see, I sent Gary pictures of my three sons, Scott, Kevin and Alan. All of them are seen as members of the Lost Boys.

CHAPTER TWENTY-FIVE

THE BOSTON BOMBERS - PART TWO

One day Leni Gronros received a letter from a convention organizer in Biloxi, Mississippi, inviting the Alpha Crew to be guests at his week-end long show. Gronros put it to all of us as to whether we wanted to go. I believe the convention folks would pick up part of the tab and Gronros would cover the rest. Everyone thought it was a great opportunity and unanimously voted to go.

While discussing the trip, we learned that the convention's big guest star would be DC writer, Mike Barr. My ears perked up at that name. Barr was well established in the field at this time and had produced several notable comics. With DC he had written the long mini-series CAMELOT 3000 which introduced American fans to the amazing British artist Brian Bolland. The series ran 12 issues long and then when completed was collected in a graphic novel format. To this day it remains one of my favorite comics.

Barr has also created a mystery comic for a smaller company entitled THE MAZE AGENCY, about a beautiful blonde private eye and her Clark Kent like friend who just happened to be a mystery writer. It was a very popular series and fans still remember it fondly.

Knowing I was going to meet Barr, I made sure to bring along my copy of the collected CAMELOT 3000 in the hopes of having him autograph it for me.

✪✪✪

When the weekend arrived, I drove up to the Portland Jetport, left my truck in the parking garage and hooked up with Gronros, Chris Mills, Bob Cram Jr. and Paul Pelletier for the flight to Mississippi. I don't recall which major airport we flew to but only that upon our arrival, we then transferred to a smaller propeller aircraft for the final leg of the journey to the coast city of Biloxi.

It was mid-summer and the weather was beautiful.

At the Biloxi airport we were picked up by one of the convention staff for the drive to the hotel where the convention was behind held. It was just after sunset when we arrived at our destination, grabbed our gear and went marching into the hotel's main lobby.

As we were doing so, Gronros spotted the fellow who was in charge. He was just walking away from the front desk with Mike Barr at his side. They spotted us and waited to greet us. The promoter quickly made the introductions.

Barr smiled and nodded upon hearing my name.

I reached out to shake his hand. "It's a pleasure to meet you, Mike."

"Same here, Ron. Now tell me, what the hell happened to the rest of the Boston Bombers?"

✪✪✪

Yup, Mike Barr was a bona fide fan of THE BOSTON BOMBERS and like most of them, he was disappointed and frustrated that the series had abruptly ended with issue number three. He wanted to know what had happened and if the last two issues had ever been published.

Putting aside my astonishment that a writer I admired so much also liked my work, I gave Barr a short Reader's Digest retelling of what had led to the series demise. I explained that our artist had mysteriously vanished off the face of the earth leaving Gary Reed with not other recourse but to cancel the series.

Barr expressed his condolences on what he called a terrific action story. With that exchange both of us began a lasting friendship.

The next few days went by fast as time always does when you are having fun. Not only was Barr gracious enough to sign my copy of CAMELOT 3000, but he also took the time to look over Paul Pelletier's portfolio. It was no surprise to the rest of the Alpha guys that he would be impressed by it. Pelletier was doing pro-quality art although he adamantly refused to submit any of his art to either Marvel or DC. His reluctance was maddening.

Barr told us he was soon to begin working on a new Batman monthly for DC to be called BATMAN AND THE OUTSIDERS and he thought Paul would be a good artist for it. We all agreed though we didn't think he had a chance in convincing Pelletier.

The Biloxi fans were truly wonderful and I also got to meet local artist Steven Butler and get reacquainted with writer Roland Mann, who I had met on my first trip to the San Diego con.

On the flight back to Maine, Gronros sat next to me. No sooner were we airborne when he asked me, "What's this Boston Bombers Mike Barr was asking about the other night?" I related the history of the project and when I was done he had a strange smile on his face.

"You think we might be able to do those last two issues?"

"Huh? What do you mean?"

"Do you still have the scripts?"

"I do."

"Then why not let us help you get them finished."

For the next twenty minutes we kicked around ideas on how that might actually be possible. The truth was no one at Alpha drew in the same style as the original artist. if I could convince Gary Kato, who had inked and lettered the first three issues, to help us out, there might be a way to get things done.

Ultimately Gary did agree and the process we came up with was convoluted but did work. Gary would take my scripts and do loose page compositions, i.e. panel layouts with light stick-figures. Then Bob Cram would complete the pencils, send the art back to Gary for final inking and lettering. It was our hope that Gary's involvement with the first three issues would allow him to maintain some of the same art-feel. And he did to a degree, God Bless him. In all our years of friendship, Gary has never once let me down. I truly owe him so much.

Driving home from Portland that Sunday evening, I was in a pretty good mood. I met one of my writing heroes, learned he liked my work and then had Gronros and the Alpha team sign on to finish the last two issues of THE BOSTON BOMBERS.

I couldn't wait to tell all this Valerie after I walked into the house. Once I finished my news, I asked how her own weekend had gone.

"Oh, the same old stuff. But you did get a call from someone named Harlan Ellison."

My heart skipped a beat. No lie.

"Who?"

"Harlan Ellison. He left his number. He wants you to call him tomorrow."

Well, the rest of that night was a lost cause in doing anything constructive. All I could do is wonder why one of the best known science fiction writers in the entire world wanted to talk to me. Known as being contentious and abrasive at times, the Hugo Award winning Ellison had achieved both success and notoriety over the years. Among the good was his having penned arguably the greatest Star Trek episode, "The City on the Edge of Forever." Another of his TV scripts was "Demon With a Glass Hand" that appeared on the classic Outer Limits.

So why was this man, whom I had never met before, suddenly want to talk to me? Suddenly I was a little kid again worrying if maybe I had done something horrible wrong and was being called about whatever so that I might be chastised and punished. Okay, so that sounds silly, but honestly, nothing like this had ever happened to me before. To the best of my knowledge, I'd done nothing to attract the attention of a public figure like Harlan Ellison. What was going on?

My world was turning upside down.

The following morning came and over breakfast Valerie asked when I was going to call him.

"I don't think I will," I said.

"What? Ron, you have to. He wants to talk to you."

"But for what?"

"You won't know that until you call him."

I hate it when she uses logic against me. It truly was an inescapable problem that could only be resolved with my acquiescing to the man's request.

I begrudgingly told her I'd call, soon as I knew it was after 9 a.m. on the west coast.

The next few hours I paced about the house until she finally told me to go sit down and stop getting in her way. I went to the living room, picked up a book and tried to read.

Two hours later I put the book down, picked up the telephone and called the number Val had been given.

There was a click on the line. "The office of Harlan Ellison," a woman's voice announced.

"Hello, this is Ron Fortier. I'm returning Mr. Ellison's call."

"Oh, right. Just a minute please."

More clicks and then …

"Fortier, what the hell happened to the Boston Bombers?"

That was the last thing in the world I was expecting to hear. Really. Especially coming on the heels of having been asked the very same question by Mike Barr not three days earlier. I mean, seriously? You go figure those odds. They are far beyond my reckoning skills.

I then proceeded to tell Mr. Ellison (he told me call him Harlan) the same sad tale I'd recounted to Barr.

"Well that's a damn shame. It is a fine comic. I enjoyed those three issues and wanted to know how it all came out."

At this point I told him about Leni Gronos's proposal which I'd agreed to and that we were going to get those last two issues completed and published as soon as possible. He was happy to hear that and I promised him once they were out, I would personally see that he received copies.

He thanked me, told me to have a good day and then hung up.

I sat on my couch, holding the phone in my hands thinking, "No one is ever going to believe this."

ADDITIONAL FACTS-

It took a few months, but eventually Gary Kato and Bob did finish the last two issues of the series. By that time I reached Gary Reed at Caliber and told him what was happening. I had no idea if he'd be willing to publish those books after so long a hiatus from when the first three had been released. But I learned Gary Reed was a man of his word and always honored his commitments. He instructed me to send him the finished pages. I did so and Caliber published a special One Shot Boston Bombers comic featuring chapters 4 & 5. Once I had copies, I immediately sent one to Mike Barr and another to Harlan Ellison.

Both Harlan Ellison and Gary Reed have since passed away. It was a honor for me to have known them.

CHAPTER TWENTY-SIX

THE RELUCTANT ARTIST

Ⓐll the while I was caught up in getting THE BOSTON BOMBERS issues wrapped up, Alpha Productions continued working on various projects. Paul Pelletier continued working on STRIKE FORCE ALPHA, shutting down any further talk about his submitting art samples to the big publishers.

The rest of us couldn't understand why he was so stubborn. His answer was always, "I'm not ready yet." Which I'm sure was sincere, but the rest of simply didn't agree with him. It was a matter where we recognized his abilities better than he did himself.

All of which led to my having a private conversation with Leni Gronros and Bob Cram about how we might trick our friend and get his work seen by somebody at Marvel. The plot was simple enough. I would write a short, 8 pg. Hulk script and tell Pelletier I'd done it strictly for exercise and then ask him, if he had the time, to draw it for me? I would swear it was just for us alone.

Then, if I managed to convince him to actually draw the strip, then Gronros would help get the pages to Cram for lettering. Once done, they would come to me and I'd submit them to Bobbie Chase; then the editor of the Hulk comic at Marvel.

It was a long shot, but somehow we actually pulled it off. I wrote a comedic story called "A Town Called Hulk," and at our next Alpha gathering, handed it to Pelletier. Of course he was suspicious at first, but when the others echoed my testimony that the strip was just for fun, he agreed to do it.

Later, when it was done, Gronros got it to Cram who wasted no time in lettering it. Then they brought the pages to me and I immediately packaged them up and sent them to Bobbie Chase who, at that time, was the editor of the Hulk monthly.

Then we all waited. All the while hoping Pelletier wouldn't ask what happened to the pages.

Approximately two weeks went by and then one night the telephone rang. Valerie picked it up, spoke a few words and then held it out to me. "It's Paul Pelletier."

I took the phone and put the receiver to my ear.

"Hi Paul."

"You son-of-a bitch!" He cursed.

In that second I knew what had happened.

"You heard from Marvel! Didn't you?"

"Yes, Bobbie Chase just called me a few minutes ago. They want to publish my Hulk story."

I was delighted and gave Valerie the thumbs up wave.

"That's great, Paul."

"Yes, I guess it is. But you shouldn't have done that behind my back."

"You're right. But Paul, this is just the beginning for you."

"You really think so?"

"Positively. They are going offer you lots more work, my friend. You can count on it."

⊙⊙⊙

Which is exactly what happened. Marvel gave him several other assignments and he delivered on all of them. Eventually word got back to Mike Barr who had wanted Pelletier to work with him on BATMAN AND THE OUTSIDERS. That also came to pass.

In no time at all Paul Pelletier was one busy professional comic book artists. In its own way, his graduating to the pros would mark the closing days of Alpha Productions.

As for our little Hulk story, it appeared in the 1989 Hulk Annual and remains to this day the one and only script I ever sold to Marvel.

ADDITIONAL FACTS ·

Although I would never sell another script to Marvel, my name did appear in the credits of two issues of THE FURTHER ADVENTURES OF INDIANA JONES. That series was written by David Michelinie and I sent him a plot idea I'd devised wherein Jones traveled to Russia and met Cossacks in his search Buffalo Bill Cody's twin gold-plated pistols. Michelinie adapted it as a two part story, gave me credit for the plot and both issues were illustrated by the legendary Steve Ditko.

CHAPTER TWENTY-SEVEN

TEKNO COMIX

So here's a comic book fairy tale for all of you. Once upon a time a lawyer couple, Lurie Silver and Mitchell Rubenstein put together a cable television network devoted solely to science-fiction. They filled the viewing hours with reruns of classic science fiction shows from the 60s and 70s. Then, because their little cable network became so popular, the USA Network came along and bought it from them for millions of dollars.

This now happy couple then packed up their bags and moved to the sunshine state of Florida with the newly acquired wealth and set about building a comic book publishing company. It would be a division of their publicly traded company called Big Entertainment.

They called it Tekno Comix and began acquiring the rights owned by big name personalities from the science fiction world. Working with Magel Barrett, the widow of the late Star Trek creator Gene Roddenberry, they developed a comic series based on one of Roddenberry's many unsold TV pilots that filled his filing cabinets. That series they called, GENE RODDENBERRY'S LOST UNIVERSE. They approached actor Leonard Nimoy, had him put together an idea and from that created LEONARD NIMOY'S PRIMORDALS. There was also ISAAC ASIMOV'S I-BOTS. By now you're getting the picture. They even contacted crime writer Mickey Spillane of Mike Hammer fame and he let them license an old comic strip idea he'd toyed with before writing his first Hammer paperback. Thus was born MICKEY SPILLANE'S MIKE DANGER; the story of a futuristic private eye tough guy.

Of course Silvers and Rubenstein had absolutely no experience in the publishing world of comics. To handle the nitty-gritty stuff, i.e. actually go out and find people to write and draw their new comic books, they required a Managing Editor. The man they hired was Ed Polgardy, a competent fellow ready to roll up his sleeves and get building this comics empire.

As the new Managing Editor of Tekno Comix, Polgardy's first job was assembling as staff of associate editors who would oversee the monthly productions of these new high profile comic series. He put out several ads in the industry papers such as the CBG and soon comic people from around the country were sending him their resumes.

One of those was Alpha's top writer, Chris Mills.

Along about the time Paul Pelletier had graduated to the ranks of a working professional graphic artist, Mills was getting anxious to get his own career moving. When he spied the notice about this newly formed comic company, he mentioned it to us to gauge our reactions. All of us, me, Gronros, Pelletier and Cram, encouraged him to contact these people and get his resume off to them. Mills is not only a damn good writer, he also loves comics and knows how to put together a creative team. Editing seem to be a natural fit for him.

Sure enough, soon after he sent Tekno his resume, he received a call from Ed Polgardy asking him to fly down to their offices for an interview. He was nervous, but again all of us urged him to go. The old adage of "nothing ventured nothing gained" applied here. He took our advice, booked his flight and off he went.

It really was no surprise to any of us when he returned home several days later with the news he'd been hired and would soon be moving to Boca Raton where the company's offices were located.

All of us were happy for him and had one final get-together to wish him well before he left Maine.

It is always wonderful to see talented people achieve their dream.

Once at Tekno, Mills met several of the other young editors recently hired by Polgordy. One of these was my friend and colleague, Martin Powell. Another was a horror writer from New York state, James Chambers.

The three of them, working under Polgardy, would form the core editorial staff and soon the new Tekno Comix titles were appearing in comic shops everywhere.

With Mills' departure, Alpha Productions was officially dead. Like so many other little comic outfits that popped up during the 80s boom, its time had come and gone like a bright shooting star across the comic heavens.

Along about this same time, I ended my relationship with Mike Friedrich and Star Reach Productions. There really wasn't need for me to have an agent by then. Without a regular series, most of my writing was devoted to my own projects and I had no idea if I'd be able to sell them or not.

ADDITIONAL FACTS ·

Years later, Friedrich left the world of comics and entered a Christian church to become an ordained minister. Funny where the roads of life lead us.

CHAPTER TWENTY-EIGHT

LOST UNIVERSE

Months flew by and I would hear from Mills every so often. He began to hint at the possibility that he might be able to get me a writing job with Tekno. I was grateful for his support and let him know I'd be available should such a position become open. It would take a few months but eventually that very opportunity presented itself.

Apparently Polgardy, under the publishers' direction, had hired a science fiction prose writer to handle GENE RODDENBERRY'S LOST UNIVERSE. In a repeat of what I'd seen happen with NOW Comics' TERMINATOR, this writer had no clue as how to write a comic book. His scripts were all talking-head dead-weights and the artist on the series was not at all happy about that. Nor was the editor, Jim Chambers.

When talk began about losing this fellow and finding a replacement, Mills stepped in and brought up my name. He elaborated on my years in the business and, of course, my work on both TERMINATOR and THE GREEN HORNET.

Polgardy directed Chambers to give me a call and see if I'd be interested. Of course, Mills called me a day earlier to tell me what had transpired and to be prepared for that call.

Like clockwork, Chambers called, introduced himself to me and then personally reported the problems they were having on LOST UNIVERSE. The artist on the book was Mike Harris and he was not the slightest bit happy with the lackluster scripts he was given to illustrate.

Chambers then went on to explain the book's main storyline. When he was done, he asked what I thought of it and how might I handle it. This was my test. Whether I won the job depended on what I said next. I didn't hesitate a second and for the next five minutes, based solely on what Chambers I had told me, I laid out what I would do with the series and characters.

When I was finished there was silence on the line. I was mentally praying a few Hail Marys.

"That sounds exactly like what the book needs," Chambers finally said. "Ron, the job is yours if you want it?'

"I do," I replied enthusiastically. "Very much."

"Alright then, what I'm going to do is make copies of Roddenberry's stuff and get it off to you via Fed Ex overnight mail.

"Okay. Soon as you get it, read it through and then start writing your first script."

"Great. I'll have it to you in a few days."

After the call, I sat back and reflected on what had just happened and what it was Jim Chambers was going to send me. I was about to read Gene Roddenberry's actual notes for his TV proposal that never happened. Okay, so that was an exciting prospect.

When the Fed Ex package arrived, I opened it up and held the thick package of papers in my hand. There was the title on the cover sheet, "THE LOST UNIVERSE, A Series Concept by Gene Roddenberry." I made myself a cup of coffee, retired to my office and sat down to read it—most carefully.

And people wonder why I love being a comic book writer.

⊕⊕⊕

After reading Roddenberry's notes, I was determined to make my scripts fast-paced and action-filled. I'd seen the previous issues and liked Mike Harris' art a great deal. I could also understand his frustration as the previous "author" had given very little to work with. In my very first script, I had a new space ship powered by giant solar-sails arrive on the scene and from that point on the action never stopped all the way to the very last page.

Upon reading it, Harris called me to welcome me happily to the book. I'd obviously given him what he wanted and from that point on we stayed in close contact while working on the series, which in itself ended up being one of the wildest such rides I've ever experienced.

At the offset, Mills had warned me that although the publishers had no idea of what they were doing, it never stopped them from poking their noses in the creators' stories. Meaning, every single script a writer turned in, after going through Polgardy's hands, had to be examined by the publishers. They in turn felt somehow qualified to make suggestions—which were not really suggestions, but orders to be carried out.

Let me clarify that a bit further.

Once on the books, Chambers and I discussed which characters would get the spotlight in the saga. That agreed upon, I then wrote my scripts accordingly. Two scripts into the storyline, one of the publishers decided we were wrong and character X should be the primary figure. Chambers then had to go back to his office, call me and explain what had happened. Out the window went the plans for the next issue and I was forced to change story direction in mid-course—to satisfy the publishers' whim.

After they read this new script, they approved it and we all breathed a sigh of relief. Chambers and I once again plotted out several issues. Then the very next month, the publishers came up with a new idea and once again, we had to change everything we were doing.

This erratic behavior became a habit until I had no clue what I would be writing from one month to the next. It was nuts! I know Chambers was as equally frustrated as I was and of course the books ultimately had no cohesiveness at all. Hell, at one point, we were told to blow up the actual planet that had been the main setting of the entire series Roddenberry had envisioned.

If you wonder how it was I was able to maintain my sanity during this crazy roller-coaster ride, the answer is simple enough. The pay was the largest per-page rate I'd ever received. In fact it was downright obscene how much money these people threw at us. Back when first bringing me into the picture, Mills had told me the operation wasn't at all well conceived and most likely would fall apart within a year. Ergo, he urged me to sign on, grab all the money I could and not worry about a long-range commitment.

His prophecy was verified as Tekno Comics didn't last for more than two years. The publishers had high hopes Hollywood would come along and option their properties thus giving them millions of dollars. Sadly their timing was off. A few film producers actually did start making overtures about the comics but it was too little too late. In the end they lost too much money and the company folded.

I was left with lots of money and bought our first big screen TV.

Thank you Tekno Comics.

ADDITIONAL FACTS •

Until her death in 2008, Majel Barrett continued to make a nice living selling her late husbands unsold projects. Once Tekno Comics folded, she took the same LOST UNIVERSE proposal we had worked on and sold it to a syndicated television producer who developed into a TV series called ANDROMEDA. It starred Kevin Sorbo and aired between 2000 and 2005.

Chris Mills returned to Maine where he continues to write and create comics.

James Chambers went back to New York and became a very successful horror writer. Only a few years later he was the recipient of the coveted Bran Stoker Award.

CHAPTER TWENTY-NINE

DAUGHTER OF DRACULA

*I*n 1931 Universal Pictures released one of the most classic horror films ever produced; "Dracula" based on the Bram Stoker novel and starring Bela Lugosi. When it premiered, the film was a big hit and naturally the studio wanted to make a sequel. Never mind that the main character is slain at the end of the movie, those kind of sticky points could easily be circumvented by imaginative screenwriters.

No, the stumbling block was Lugosi who refused to do it. Having played the famous bloodsucker on stage for many years, it was always his intention to culminate that association with the movie. After which he would move on to other parts.

Universal was stymied and it wouldn't be until 1936 when they revisited the idea of a sequel and released "Dracula's Daughter." The film begins within minutes of the first movie's ending with Dracula's daughter, Marya Zaleska, arriving in England to claim her father's remains. She then burns the corpse on a fiery funeral pyre in the countryside.

Believing her own vampirism is a mental disorder, she seeks the help of Dr. Jeffrey Garth, a well-known London psychiatrist in the hopes he can cure her of the malady. Of course that never happens. In the end Marya not only comes to accept her cursed immortal fate but attempts to turn Garth into one of the undead so that they both may live forever.

Actress Gloria Holden was under studio contract and given the lead. According to film historians, she wasn't happy about the assignment fearing, like Bugosi before her, she too would be typecast in horror films. Which is ironic as Ms. Holden possessed a dark, seductive beauty and her reluctance seems to have enhanced her performance as a tortured soul throughout the movie. Veteran actor Otto Kruger played Dr. Garth who is at first mesmerized by her exotic beauty and then repulsed by her true nature.

Years later critics are still fairly divided with half saying the film is slow and ponderous while those who applaud it point out its erotic undertones. Repressed sexuality has always been an element in vampire lore what with the sophisticated male count giving his beautiful victim the ultimate hickey. While in "Dracula's Daughter" you had a beautiful mature woman doing the same to a lovely younger girl.

Hot stuff indeed for a 1936 flick.

I don't remember exactly when I first saw "Dracula's Daughter." Most likely on one of those midnight horror television shows that were so popular in 50s and 60s. I was in my teens and it left a lasting impression on me. Enough so that whenever I knew it was going to be scheduled, I'd make sure to watch it again.

By the time I was an adult "Dracula's Daughter" was one of my favorite movies, enough so that for many years I entertained hopes of one day getting to write Marya myself.

That opportunity would come about ironically because of another Universal monster film. This one a whole lot different than "Dracula's Daughter."

❂❂❂

In 1999 Universal released "The Mummy" starring Brendan Frasier. It was a very radical reboot of the early 1932 horror classic that had starred Boris Karloff as the resurrected Egyptian priest, Imhotep. Whereas, in this remake, the story revolved around a world trotting adventurer cast in the mold of Indiana Jones crossing paths with the reawakened monster now played by Arnold Vosloo.

It was a pulpish mash up of two genres; the traditional horror yarn and the rousing adventure story. Honestly, most fans who saw it quickly labeled it Indiana Jones vs The Mummy and that is exactly what it was.

As odd as that mash-up sounds, it worked to storytelling perfection and was a huge hit that went on to have two sequels and spawn a separate spin-off series called "The Scorpion King."

I personally loved that flick and months after seeing it began wondering how I could similarly utilize Marya by placing her in a totally fresh and different setting. It didn't take me long to come up with such a background. I've been a fan of aviation history for most of my life and was always fascinated by aviation combat pilots of World War One. How brave those men were for going up in those cheaply constructed aircraft made of paper and wood. They fought incredible aerial duels high above the trenches.

The greatest of these Flying Knights was the German ace, Manfred von Richthofen who gained fame as the Red Baron.

One day, while surfing the internet, I began researching Richthofen's life and career. A thought crept into my head very slowly. What if just prior to the start of that war, he would cross paths with the beautiful Marya von Dracula and she

became enamored of him. Keeping in mind that by this time she would have been five hundred years old. Five centuries of living alone in a Transalvanian castle with only a few servants to tend to her needs. Feeding off the blood of her victims and enduring a bleak, loveless existence.

Then one night, while riding through the woods on her estate, she meets this handsome, virile German lad and falls headlong in love with him.

It was all I needed to start plotting what would become a 108 page graphic novel I'd titled, DAUGHTER OF DRACULA.

The process by how I wrote it was this. I wrote a detailed timeline of Richthofen's life from his youth to his entering the service, becoming a flier, then an ace all the way to his eventual death. I put this sheet on the desk along side my computer making sure to keep the historical aspects intact. Then I wove the fantasy love story around those dates.

In the book Marya waits several years until Manfred has become a flying hero and then she travels to Berlin to seduce him. They have a torrid love affair and eventually he learns that she is a vampire. At first he is disgusted by it, but in the end cannot overcome his obsessive passion for her. He agrees to let her administer the vampire's kiss and thus turn him into an undead creature as well. This is done by her draining him almost to the point of death two times. Then with the third such "kiss" he dies and is buried only to rise again the following night.

As the story progresses Marya gives him the first kiss and then nurses him back to health. A few weeks later she repeats the process. Upon regaining his health, Manfred has to return to his squadron and combat but promises to return soon whereby she will give him the third and final "kiss."

Alas, it is during this period when, according to the actual timeline I was using, he is killed in action and never returns to her. When Marya is informed of his death, she goes mad and begins her own supernatural campaign against the Allied flying forces. It is brutal and savage. She sends armies of rats to invade their airfields and hangars while commanding thousand of flying bats to bring down their aircrafts.

At which point something happens which turns the entire tale upside down. This twist has surprised hundreds of readers in the past ten years. Sorry, but if you want to know the secret ending of DAUGHTER OF DRACULA, you're just going to go out and pick up a copy.

Ain't I a meany?

000

Having finished the script, I then began the arduous task of sending out inquiries to the various comic publishers in hopes of finding one to buy the darn thing. I failed every single time. Not one single company would take a chance on my romantic horror thriller.

As time went on and I related this annoyance to several of my colleagues, some of them began to suggest the story might work better as a film. They urged me to rewrite it as a screenplay.

Eventually I did just that. Now I had both a graphic novel and screenplay version of DAUGHTER OF DRACULA and still I couldn't get anyone to bite. (Pun intended.)

Five years elapsed and then one night, while surfing the internet I came across a comic website being maintained by an old artist friend.

It turned out to be one of the luckiest moments in my life.

CHAPTER THIRTY

REDBUD STUDIO

By the time I wrote DAUGHTER OF DRACULA, I'd experience enough ups and downs in the comic book game that unsold projects no longer bothered me all that much. Thus during the five years the script languished in my files, I wrote other things. One of those was a three act play about how my parents had met and fallen in love during World War II called "Where Love Takes You."

The play was produced by a small community theater group in Sanford, Maine and on opening night Mom was seated front row center surrounded by my siblings. I'd like to think Dad had a balcony seat in heaven.

Shortly afterwards both Valerie and I retired from General Electric after thirty years of service. Living on a very nice pension and having flexed my creative muscles by writing a play, I then began to try my hand at writing pulp short stories. Moonstone Comics had started publishing prose anthologies and Editor Joe Gentile invited me to contribute to several of them. Thus I wrote short stories of the Phantom, the Green Hornet and the pulp characters the Spider and the Avenger. It was the beginning of a whole new career for me as a writer.

✪✪✪

One evening, while seated at my PC surfing the internet, I stumbled upon a web-comic called "The Spirit of 66" as written and illustrated by my old correspondent pal, Rob Davis. I pulled it up on my screen and saw it was done in strip form ala the traditional newspaper cartoons but here the panels were done to fit a typical square computer screen.

The title referred to the old U.S. Route 66 that had one time been the major transcontinental highway of the USA. The story was about a young man who, upon his father's passing, inherits the old man's '66 Thunderbird. He decides to take it on a cross-country trip using the "mother road" and ultimately discovers that the car is actually haunted by the ghost of his father; who in turns leads the hero into various adventures.

Rob did everything on the strip; write, draw, letter and color. I was impressed but not at all surprised. He'd always been a fantastic artist and it was heartening to see that his art had only improved over the years since we'd been in touch.

Fortunately the site had Rob's e-mail address and I wrote him immediately. I gave him a short rundown on my own current situation and inquired as to how he was doing since we'd last had contact with each other.

In his reply, Rob related how he'd been let go from Malibu after the early 90s industry implosion. A whole lot of talented people had lost their jobs when that inflated boom collapsed. Rather than spend time looking for other assignments that were becoming fewer and fewer, Rob bit the bullet and took a job as a bus driver for the city of Columbia, Missouri. He had a family and responsibilities to take care of.

Still the urge to create was too strong to resist completely which led him to create "The Spirit of 66." He ended his letter asking if I was doing anything comics-wise myself.

In my reply, I told him about DAUGHTER OF DRACULA. Rob was intreigued and asked if there was a digital script, could he read it. Took me all of three minutes to send him the digital copy along with a note saying I hoped he would enjoy it.

A few days went by then he wrote back. He said he liked the script a great deal and it was something he felt he could have fun drawing. Unfortunately with his current obligations, the best he could do on such a project would be one page a week. Considering the script was 108 pages long, Rob logically assumed there was no way I would want to wait over two years to see the book done.

What he hadn't taken into account were two very important factors. One, he was offering to pencil, ink and letter the entire graphic novel. All 108 pages. I honestly don't think Rob realized just how much a fan of his work I really was… and remain so to this day. He is a gifted artist. The opportunity to have him be the artist on this book was just too good to say no to. Secondly, I'd already waited five years for something to happen. What was another two?

Thus he was genuinely surprised when I responded, "Alright. Let's do it."

ADDITIONAL FACTS·

Rob's being "let go" from Malibu was actually a side-effect of the consolidation of the comics industry after the comics implosion of the mid to late 1990s. Marvel Comics purchased Malibu and its subsidiaries ostensibly in an attempt to get its ground-breaking in-house digital coloring staff in the Marvel stable. However, the coloring staff stymied the attempt by jumping ship and going freelance.

For a while Malibu was left alone but eventually Marvel acquired the rights to all the Star Trek licenses (DC had, until that point had Star Trek and Star Trek: The Next Generation while Malibu had Star Trek: Deep Space Nine. The latter was the title Rob did most of his later work at Malibu) and brought them under their banner. At the same time they dissolved Malibu and canceled all its titles. For some unknown reason the editor of the new Trek books at Marvel decided that no creators who had worked on the books prior to Marvel's tenure would be hired for the new books under their masthead. Thus Rob and a good number of other comics creators were left high and dry in a shrinking field…

For the next two years Rob was true to his word. Every single week he would do a new page and send them to me digitally. Every single one was so damn beautiful, I was constantly pinching myself. Of course life isn't always easy and there were times when circumstances made it impossible for him to deliver that weekly page. When those few times did occur, Rob let me know and the following week he would produce two pages instead of one. He was determined to stay on his on set schedule.

Exactly two years and four weeks later, Rob Davis turned in the final page of our graphic novel. I wanted to shout out loud; I was that happy. What really had wowed me was how Rob never once lost his own enthusiasm for the story. One would figure after twenty, thirty, forty…weeks, his interest might wane. He just might have gotten tired with it all and thus illustrated subpar pages every so often. That never happened once. Not one time. Every single 108 pages of DAUGHTER OF DRACULA is Rob Davis at his finest and each shines as a perfect example of what a comic page should look like.

To this day I consider it his masterpiece.

Now that the graphic novel was finished, I expected us to sell it quickly once we began showing samples around. We put together small presentation packages with outlines of the plot and a few of Rob's beautiful pages and sent them out across the internet to well-known publishers.

Every one of them turned it down.

That's when it dawned on me that the comic world had really gone off the deep end. While Marvel and DC continued to publish the same old stories, they became deaf, dumb and blind to anything new and of quality. None of this bode well for the industry.

Rob was equally frustrated and after the umpteenth rejection, made the decision that we should just publish it ourselves.

Always fascinated by new technology, Rob had taught himself things like desktop publishing and was very aware of the new on-demand printing houses popping up all over the internet. One of these was an outfit called Ka-Blam owned and operated by veteran comics writer Barry Gregory.

Rob told me he could assemble DAUGHTER OF DRACULA digitally and then for a small fee post it at Ka-Blam. From that point on we would simply have to order copies from them whenever we were going to a convention. There was no need for a standing inventory ever. We would be masters of our own destiny.

I thought it was a super idea and supported it. While Rob started putting the files together, I went out and recruited painter Mark Maddox to do a color cover based on my composition idea. I had him show a young woman's torso wearing a tight bustier that shows off her ample charm. Hanging from the neck over her bosom is the Blue Max, the award given German fliers when they became aces. The image rises up to the woman's mouth where we see her fangs over her luscious red lips….and nothing else. We do not see beyond that point.

Maddox argued with me initially that not showing Marya's eyes was a mistake. Wherein my rebuttal was that if we saw all of her head the picture would simply morph into just another sexy cheesecake type of art. By focusing on her fangs, bosom and that pendant, my intent was to visually show her monstrous sexuality.

We comprised by having Maddox do a full painting, then crop it for our cover. He kept the full image and made postcards of it. He hoped to make poster size prints at a later date with our blessings. When he finally saw a printed copy, he dropped that idea and admitted I'd been right all along. The cover delivered exactly what I'd wanted it to.

Rob and I began taking copies to the various conventions we were attending and the book began to sell. Knowing our old friend Tony Isabella wrote an online comics review column, I sent him a copy. When reviewing it, Tony gave it major thumbs up comparing it to an old Hammer horror movie.

That was over ten years ago. In that time span, Rob and I have sold hundreds of copies of DAUGHTER OF DRACULA.

Oh, and I almost forgot. Just prior to putting the finishes touches on the cover,

Rob realized he should have a name for this new comics venture. Thus he called his new outfit Redbud Studio.

○○○

The success of getting DAUGHTER published only encouraged us to do more of our own comics via Redbud.

First up was the idea of collecting all the Mr. Jigsaw stories that had been published over the past thirty years and reprinting them in what would be Jiggy's own black and white comics series. With Gary Kato's help, we were able to find decent copies of all those old stories and when adding them realized they would fill three 24 page issues.

Once MR. JIGSAW – Man of a Thousand Parts 1 to 3 were printed via Redbud Studio, I began writing newer stories. Today we've done 15 issues and number 16 is in production.

Rob also reprinted ROBYN OF SHERWOOD, a series he'd done with writer Paul Storrie many, many years ago. Steadily we were building a nice catalog of Redbud Studio titles. Remember those old Rambo scripts I mentioned earlier, well they were now turned into THE BLACK LION, a new black hero and the art was being draw by veteran Army sergeant Kevin Johnson.

I even managed to get an anthology series of horror and fantasy tales with my own name on it, RON FORTIER'S TALES OF THE MACABRE. We've done 6 of those to date.

One day I approached Rob about possibly assembling all the issues of BOSTON BOMBERS into one big book. It posed problems, but in the end, just like MR. JIGSAW, we managed to get our hands on all the pages and Rob pulled it off. One of our good friends, sci-fi writer Van Allen Plexico, was kind enough to write an introduction to it. What surprised me the most was that after he'd read it all, Rob asked me to write an afterword. BOSTON BOMBERS, as much as DAUGHTER OF DRACULA, is a constant seller at all our conventions. Since then Rob has also collected those online SPIRIT OF ROUTE 66 pages into a comic book including a never before published Rt. 66 story by writer Jeff Limke and an all new "Tales of the Mother Road" story by me and illustrated by Rob.

It was all too clear by now that the future of comics rested in the independents such as what we were doing with Redbud. Digital comics and on-demand printing were changing the face of American comics forever.

ADDITIONAL FACTS ·

Several years after publishing DAUGHTER OF DRACULA, Rob and I were invited to the Oklahoma Fiction Writers Conference in Norman, OK. This is an annual invitational and conference boasting over eight hundred members. The governing committee had received multiple requests from their members to have creators familiar with graphic novels be guests at the convention to present workshops on the format. Luckily one of those on the committee had a relative who happened to be an acquaintance and he gave them our names. Thrilled by the invitation, we immediately put together a 90 minute workshop. I would open it and discuss the differences between writing comics and prose for the first 30 minutes. Then Rob would do a slide show using pages from DAUGHTER OF DRACULA to show how he, as the artist, interpreted my script pages. Then we'd leave the last 30 minutes for questions from our audience.

In all, it seemed like a good plan. Then, about a month before the conference, it dawned on me that we be sharing almost 90 yrs of experience in the comics business in those two workshops. That's a whole lot of lessons to be exposed to in so little a time. I realized that most of those attending our workshops would most likely forget half of what we would be telling them by the time they returned home. So, how to solve that problem?

I called Rob and expressed my concerns and then asked if it would be possible to print my actual manuscript? Rob said he could do that easily enough and he'd even design it with individual panels from the graphic novel to dress it up. He did just that and by the time we arrived in Norman, we had copies of both the comic and the printed manuscript book. Thus attendees leaving the workshop were able to buy both and then cross-reference them any time they wished. A writer reading my manuscript and curious as to how Rob had drawn a particular page could simply pick up the graphic novel and see that. Inversely a writer reading the graphic novel and intrigued by a particular page of art, ala its composition and layout could then pick up the manuscript book and see how I had written that particular page. Thus these volumes became a one-two teaching tool for anyone wishing to learn how to write comics and graphic novels.

CHAPTER THIRTY-ONE

PAYING IT BACK

Ever since moving to Fort Collins, Colorado, I've sensed a new chapter of my career taking hold of my time and interests. Early on I found that the locale is filled with many comic professionals, both writers and artists and many, many fans. Delighted by this, I, along with several area friends began an informal comics club that meets once a month.

As expected, the group continues to grow every year until our roster is over thirty strong.

While all this was transpiring, I began to think of what it might be like to teach a class in comics scripting. After a couple of years, I set my sights on a nearby institution called the Front Range Community College. One day I emailed the Director of the Continuing Adult Education program. This is the branch in most colleges that offers night classes to people in the community in all kinds of subjects.

Months passed and I began to think my inquiry had disappeared in an internet black hole. Then one morning there was this email from Laurie Rue, the Director of said program at Front Range. She was excited about my suggestion to teach a class in comic writing and invited me to meet with her to discuss the possibility in detail.

That was two years ago and since then I have taught my ten week course four times. In my first class I had five students, three in my second, seven in my third and now four in the current course. The experience has been supremely reward-ing for me and I have had so much fun in sharing the things I've learned with my students. The joy of a night class environment is the diversity of the students who sign on. I've had adults, college students and last year a 13 year old young lady who was joy to work with.

All of which amazes me at just how widespread is today's comic fandom. All of my students have been eager to learn, to write and to make comics.

As I get deeper into my senior adventures, teaching this class has been a true gift to my spirit. Over the many years of my career I've been blessed with great teachers, mentors, and editors. All of whom helped guide me along. I see teaching as a way for me to pay them back. I hope I can do it for many years to come.

CHAPTER THIRTY-TWO

SO, WHAT'S NEXT?

It looks like we're finally coming to the end of this story. When I look back through all these pages and the tales I've finally put on paper, I'm a little awed by how fast the past 68 years of my life have sped by. Consider Chapter One and I'm all of five years old and now I'm about to turn 73 in just a few weeks.

If you take anything away from this book it's just how big a part of my life's journey comic books have really been. It has been a remarkable trip and I am so grateful to all the people I've met along the way; yes, even those one might consid-er antagonistic. I think it's impossible to live as long as I have and not have pissed off a few people along the way. I wish that weren't so and I truly regret any harm or pain I may have caused anyone. Whether they choose to forgive me or not is up to them.

To all my friends, family, colleagues who have become a part of this story in such positive ways, my heartfelt thanks. No one lives a solitary life and mine has truly been blessed by such beautiful souls.

A special thanks goes to artists Gary Kato, Jeff Butler and Rob Davis; my three amigos.

So what's on the table? Well Gary and I plan on continuing the funny adventures of Mr. Jigsaw as long as we are able. In fact a giant sized, full color issue #16 is now in production and hopefully we'll have it out by Christmas this year. A tip of the hat to artist Mort Todd who provided the lush colors.

Artist Cesar Feliciano, formerly of Massachusetts and now a Florida guy, hooked me into doing a new action thriller comic he titles JIN & TONIK. It's about two assassins, one Chinese and the other Russian and I have had a ball working on the first few chapters. Cesar's hope is to fund the series via an on-line funding program ala Kickstarter some time in 2020 so keep your eyes out for it.

Ever since doing DAUGHTER OF DRACULA together, Rob and I have wanted to do another project together. As he loved the first BOSTON BOMBERS series, he suggested I sit down and pen the second saga. Upon reading the first, Rob was smart to realize there was a whole lot more story to tell. With fingers crossed, we'll be working on BOSTON BOMBERS TWO as soon as time allows.

And after those, who knows. I'm sure the muse will zap me again soon enough. It has never let me down yet.

Speaking of that muse, this seems like a very good segue into our last chapter.

CHAPTER THIRTY-THREE

THE LAST STORY

Way back before I could possibly imagine the career I would someday have, I struggled with the idea that I would ever succeed. After having completed the STREET-FIGHTER series for Bob Palin and Ocean Comics, I hit what seemed like an insurmountable wall of rejections. Every new proposal I sent out was quickly returned with a big old "No thanks" affixed to it.

Week and months followed and no one wanted my stories. I fell into a black funk and one day, out of sheer frustration announced to Valerie that I was all done with writing. All it was giving me was nothing but disappointment. It seemed like my dreams would never come true and the road ahead would be filled with nothing by heartache.

Ergo, why bother? I was done. Finished. Time to move on to a normal life without writing or comics.

✪✪✪

At that time we belonged to a beautiful little Catholic church community in Rollingsford, NH called Saint Mary's. I was a Lector and found great satisfaction in reading from the bible at mass services. That year the midnight mass was a truly wonderful event and our little church was packed not only with our parishioners but lots of their families visiting from out of town.

The mass was truly wonderful and after it ended, many of us gathered in the entrance vestibule to wish each other Merry Christmas. I looked out the door and saw that it had started to snow lightly. The street outside, lit by the streetlamps looked like a Currier & Ives painting brought to life.

Valerie was having an animated chat with friends and I interrupted her to say I was going out to the parking lot and get our car. Then I'd drive around to the front of the building to pick her up. She smiled, acknowledged that and I headed out into the cold night.

I was weaving my way to our car through the quiet lot when a voice called out to me.

"Mr. Fortier!"

I turned around to see a young boy of about ten rushing up to me. He was smartly dressed in a suit and tie and looked very happy.

"Yes?"

He stopped in front of me. "My name's Tom. I'm Bea Landry's grandson from Texas." Mrs. Landry was a friend and fellow employee at the G.E. plant where Valerie and I worked. "She sent me all your Street-Fighter comics. I think they're the best comics ever. I really liked them a lot."

"Thank you," I stammered.

"You're welcome. Merry Christmas!"

And off he went to find his family leaving me standing there, snow falling on my head, in the middle of that church parking lot. What that young boy had said echoed in my heart and I knew who had sent him to me on that Christmas night.

I looked up at the stars twinkling through the delicate snowflakes.

"Thank you, God."

I never thought of quitting again.

RON FORTIER – Comics and pulps writer/editor best known for his work on the Green Hornet comic series and Terminator – Burning Earth with Alex Ross. He won the Pulp Factory Award for Best Pulp Short Story of 2011 for "Vengeance Is Mine," which appeared in Moonstone's The Avenger – Justice Inc. and in 2012 for "The Ghoul," from the anthology Monster Aces. He was named Pulp Grand Master by the Pulp Factory group in 2017. He is the Managing Editor of Airship 27 Productions, a New Pulp Fiction publisher and writes the continuing adventures of both his own character, Brother Bones – the Undead Avenger and the classic pulp hero, Captain Hazzard – Champion of Justice.

ROB DAVIS - began his professional art career doing illustrations for role-playing games in the late 1980's. Soon after he began lettering and inking then penciling comics for a number of small black and white comics publishers— most notably for Eternity Comics, which eventually became Malibu Comics in the 1990's. He established his comics credentials on Eternity's black and white comic book SCIMIDAR with writer R.A. Jones. Eventually working at both DC and Marvel Rob specialized in likeness intensive comics like adaptations of TV shows QUANTUM LEAP and STAR TREK's many incarnations, mostly on the DEEP SPACE NINE comics for Malibu. At Marvel he worked on the Saturday morning cartoon adaptation to comics of PIRATES OF DARK WATER. After the comics industry implosion in the late 1990s Rob picked up work on video games, advertising illustration and T-shirt design as well as some small press comics like ROBYN OF SHERWOOD for Caliber. Rob continues to do the occasional self-published comic book as well as publisher and designer for his small-press production studio REDBUD STUDIO COMICS. Rob is Art Director, Designer and Illustrator for the New Pulp production outfit AIRSHIP 27 partnered with writer/editor Ron Fortier. Rob is the recipient of the PULP FACTORY AWARD for "Best Interior Illustrations" in 2010 and 2016 for his work on SHERLOCK HOLMES: CONSULTING DETECTIVE and has been nominated for the same award every year since its inception. He works and lives in central Missouri with his wife and two children.

You can find examples of his work at robmdavis.com.

Made in the USA
Middletown, DE
28 March 2024

51873507R00060